Boundary Images

IN SEARCH OF MEDIA

Timon Beyes, Mercedes Bunz, and
Wendy Hui Kyong Chun, Series Editors

Boundary Images

Giselle Beiguelman, Melody Devries,
Winnie Soon, and Magdalena Tyżlik-Carver

IN SEARCH OF MEDIA

University of Minnesota Press
Minneapolis
London

meson press

In Search of Media is a collaboration between the University of Minnesota Press and meson press, an open access publisher, https://meson.press.

Published by the University of Minnesota Press, 2023
111 Third Avenue South, Suite 290
Minneapolis, MN 55401-2520
https://www.upress.umn.edu

in collaboration with
meson press
Salzstrasse 1
21335 Lüneburg, Germany
https://meson.press

ISBN 978-1-5179-1612-1 (pb)
Library of Congress record available at https://lccn.loc
.gov/2023024434

Contents

Series Foreword

"Media determine our situation," Friedrich Kittler infamously wrote in his Introduction to *Gramophone, Film, Typewriter.* Although this dictum is certainly extreme—and media archaeology has been critiqued for being overly dramatic and focused on technological developments—it propels us to keep thinking about media as setting the terms for which we live, socialize, communicate, organize, do scholarship, et cetera. After all, as Kittler continued in his opening statement almost thirty years ago, our situation, "in spite or because" of media, "deserves a description." What, then, are the terms—the limits, the conditions, the periods, the relations, the phrases—of media? And, what is the relationship between these terms and determination? This book series, *In Search of Media,* answers these questions by investigating the often elliptical "terms of media" under which users operate. That is, rather than produce a series of explanatory keyword-based texts to describe media practices, the goal is to understand the conditions (the "terms") under which media is produced, as well as the ways in which media impacts and changes these terms.

Clearly, the rise of search engines has fostered the proliferation and predominance of keywords and terms. At the same time, it has changed the very nature of keywords, since now any word and pattern can become "key." Even further, it has transformed the very process of learning, since search presumes that, (a) with the right phrase, any question can be answered and (b) that the answers lie within the database. The truth, in other words, is "in there." The impact of search/media on knowledge, however, goes beyond search engines. Increasingly, disciplines—from sociology to economics, from the arts to literature—are in search of media as a way to revitalize their methods and objects of study. Our current media situation therefore seems to imply a new term, understood as temporal shifts of mediatic conditioning. Most broadly, then, this series asks: What are the terms or conditions of knowledge itself?

To answer this question, each book features interventions by two (or more) authors, whose approach to a term—to begin with: *communication, pattern discrimination, markets, remain, machine, archives, organize, action at a distance, undoing networks*—diverges and converges in surprising ways. By pairing up scholars from North America and Europe, this series also advances media theory by obviating the proverbial "ten year gap" that exists across language barriers due to the vagaries of translation and local academic customs and in order to provoke new descriptions, prescriptions, and hypotheses—to rethink and reimagine what media can and must do.

Introduction

Boundary Images

Melody Devries, Magdalena Tyżlik-Carver, Winnie Soon, and Giselle Beiguelman

Assemblages and Infrastructures: Continuing beyond Representation

As four different authors—artists, curators, theorists, and anthro-pologists—we have sought to push the boundaries of what it means to go beyond representation within the study of images. While many philosophers and media theorists have prompted media researchers to move beyond representation, (e.g. Ahmed 2008; Braidotti 2002; Parikka and Sampson 2009; Paasonen 2011), what this move actually looks like is something that warrants further exploration and experimentation. This is the challenge we have sought to take up in this book, expanding the inquiry from the perspective of different disciplinary and geographic positions. Images exist in techno-social ecologies of computational networks that automate production and circulation of the visual. When writing these chapters, we have found ourselves asking how we might approach visual productions of the world in a way that centers the material relations that both create and involve images as actants themselves. In part inspired by new materialist imaginings, art and digital media, and political insurgencies, we've found ourselves asking: How do the various codes that present us with images per-form politically? Furthermore, what happens when we analyze not only visual elements but also account for images' vibrance (Bennet

2010), the lives and loves of those images (Mitchell 2005), and the biases of images (Pasquinelli and Joler 2020)?

The chapters in this book present widely varied approaches to these questions but are united in their shared move to present tangible experiments in analyzing images beyond representation while not leaving such representations behind. To us, images are both assemblages and infrastructures for crossing between geopolitical and ontological purviews, and not always to positive ends. This is where a shared consideration of boundary image becomes useful, as it allows us to dissect the images, their vibrance, and—most importantly here—the related elements of the dispersed networks within which images live and act. For Susan Leigh Star and James R. Griesemer (1989), a boundary object is an entity that links networks, elastic enough to be adapted to a new context and robust enough to keep its main characteristics. Coming together over the boundary image thus allows us to highlight the networked and formative activity of images within social, political, and technical contexts, and in the process to account for their political effects. In this sense, these chapters share the assertion that boundary images of any kind and the crossings they facilitate must be considered as political phenomena, as they are connected with systems that reproduce state, ideological, technological, and material relations of power, if even in mundane moments and spaces. Launching from these shared epistemologies, terminologies, and goals, we present a volume that investigates boundary images from different disciplinary positions: from that of the artist and curator, media theorist, and anthropologist. This allows *Boundary Images* to widely interrogate the activity of images as it is generated and circulated from various lively elements: moving parts and algorithmic codes, symbols, ideologies, or emotions and bodies. In the end, we attest that this seeming disciplinary disparity is itself representative of the potential for both the concept of boundary images and the practical move beyond representation to have applications for different modalities of research into the involvement of images within contemporary political phenomena.

This book interrogates and circumvents the spatial and temporal boundaries between media networks, power and empowerment, humans, nonhumans, and their various interpretations of and experiences with the world. Boundaries and borders are always productive, if in constitutive but not emancipatory ways. The language, uptake, and creation of borders and boundaries—whether between "us and them," "visible and invisible," or "real and fake"—inevitably present a global politics that operates through static objectivities, hierarchies of legitimacy, and laws of the state. The active relations that form borders and boundaries value familiarity and consistency, even (or especially) when presented with new probes. It is this active quality of boundary in forming or allowing access to various realities of nation-state, ontology, or humanness that makes the study of boundary images so fruitful. Boundary images, like boundary objects, allow or deny access based on who is eligible to take them up. While boundaries reify distinctions (be it harmful or positive) in and about the world, we have found that art and images provide evidence of how they are either established, maintained, or surpassed.

In these chapters, going beyond representation to study images as involved in boundary maintenance and crossing has meant also moving beyond dichotomic distinctions between the symbolic and the affective and vibrant, the latter being the capacity of things or images to not only exert influence on the human body but be capable of being changed by human and nonhuman agents. In her book *Vibrant Matter* (2010), Jane Bennett critiques the habit of parsing the world into two categories: dull matter and vibrant life. Such a division is an ontological move that conceptualizes agency and action as located within moving, thinking beings, and between those who have no ability to take part in the perceptually real. The study of imagery and representation has in the past endured a similar partition between the lively and the static via the distinction made between the affective and the textual. As this turn has been described (Paasonen 2011), analysis of the lively image has been one that attends to how images produce affective intensities and how an image may be material and dynamic, while textual analysis conceives of a static image that presents semiotics and evokes ideology, meaning, and significations. In this dichotomy, it is not matter and materiality that are conceived as dull, but the immaterial signifiers, composed of lively texts, tubes, colors, code, and data.

Scholars have provided a necessary critique of the textual turn as treating meaning as always already fixed-in-place when presented within an image or text. As Susanna Paasonen explains and to which Bennett's work speaks, any approach that presumes meaning-making to be located only in the already-presented (i.e. fixed) "representation" of the material brings forth a certain "tyr-anny of the semantic at the cost of the sensory and the material" (Paasonen 2011, 9).

At the same time, focusing on what is lively should not need to alienate the textual. To do so is what replicates an unnecessary partition between static visible texts and lively affective renderings. As has been pointed out by Claire Hemmings (2005), Sara Ahmed (2008), and others, the idea of a turn away from the sedentary, the philosophical, or the abstract and instead toward the lively dynamism of the material is to maintain a binary logic that marks one perspective as negative, stifled, and the other as morally ascendant in its embrace of life and liveliness. More importantly, these critiques reject the absolute staticity of representation and symbol, and considers these as also lively alongside the materiality of the image. These apt critiques push scholarship on images to move beyond attempts to separate affective analysis of images from textual analysis (Paasonen 2011) and to incorporate both computational networked infrastructure and meaning into our assessment of how images and their representations form and move between people, technology, and worlds (Chun 2008; Parikka and Sampson 2009; Dewdney and Sluis 2022).

In some sense, this double perception of images,—both at their lively parts and their supposedly fixed meanings—might resemble

what W. J. T. Mitchell (2005, 7) defines as the "double consciousness" that Western imaginaries have when perceiving images.
Seeing with this double consciousness, the viewer is able to be
simultaneously skeptical of images' ability to act, while at the same
time attribute to them the ability to move or act upon the gullible;
to influence, to move, to animate (Mitchell 2005). Such thinking
about and ability to be influenced by images has historically been
attributed to nonwhite folk, non-Westerners, children, women,
"the masses, the illiterate, the uncritical, the illogical, the 'Other,'"
whereas the critical or skeptical view of images as representations is held by those who are "modern" and can look "behind"
those images (Mitchell 2005). Of course, Mitchell asserts that the
"modern world" (meaning the white, Western European world)
has never interacted solely rationally or skeptically with images,
hence the double consciousness that recognizes the agency of
images but doesn't attribute such "magical thinking" to itself. In
following Mitchell's assertion that the so called "modern" minds
are not superior to the so-called "nonmodern," these chapters pay
attention to what is in and around the picture in order to forward
and act on the assertion that the animacy, vibrancy, and worldmaking capacities of images are something that should be taken
seriously (see chapter 2). This challenge to take seriously the lives
and relations of images is what we attempt in the chapters that
follow, while approaching the internet and technology from very
different starting points, which Chun calls an important inevitability
of studying the effects of new media and digital technologies (Chun
2008, 299–300).

It is worth following such prompts in our contemporary context,
given the growth of cultural studies that have revised elements of
the textual turn via discursive analysis in response to the resur-
gence of far-right movements globally (Hughes 2019; Venturini
2021), as well as those accounts that might attribute gullible thinking to the political or "repugnant other" (Lennon 2018; Harding
1991). By working beyond both representation and affect, and
by embracing the somewhat magical agencies of images, these

6   chapters forward an analytical practice that takes seriously the intense multifaceted texture of assemblages of cultural production. In this book, culture, politics, affect, belief, software, textual content, and semantics are interwoven with networks that link ideology and fantastical belief with social-media infrastructures, machine-learning sequences with biological life, and violent political histories with glaring absence. In this sense, we define images as lively, illusive assemblages of moving parts, histories, and symbols that variedly run into and alongside humans and other entities.

Importantly, our thinking of images as living is not meant to anthropomorphize them in order to understand them, nor to think of them as solely confined to the material. Rather, we explore images as relational entities with vibrant borders. Indeed, boundary images are precisely those images whose network capacity prevents their staticity. This book on boundary images investigates these different relations as each essay follows specific images and image categories to dissect the lives of these images and to see what kind of world they are part of making. The three essays offer analyses of images as part of wider ecologies where a multiplicity of relations—historical, procedural, and between people and technologies, people and things, and ways of knowing and being in the world—can be traced through in-depth inquiry into the boundaries and borders that these images help cross and create.

Collectively, then, we ask: How might our understanding of the relationship between images, politics, and technology change when we take seriously the deeply relational vitality of images as simultaneously affective, textual, political, cultural, algorithmic, and mechanical? How does this alter how we approach understanding the nationalist and populist politics encountered in the volatile contexts of absence and imminent becoming presented in each chapter? How is colonialism updated, reinforced, and even embraced within new forms of domination facilitated by socio-technological networks? In the end, this book is not about boundaries nor images exactly but about the ways that images in their technical materiality, their affective powers, and their textual semantics reproduce violent borders while also creating roadmaps for travel through and beyond boundaries.

The Politics of Boundary Images

The book's central concept, the boundary image, draws from Susan Leigh Star's (1989; 2010) concept of the boundary object. Contrary to the potential implications of its name as a marker of boundary, the boundary object is the exact opposite of 'an end' or marker of strict impermeability. Rather, a boundary object is a thing, entity, or any other type of object that can be shared or used differently by varying groups, with each holding its own representation, understanding, or normative practices with that object (Star and Greisemer 1989). Via its capacity to be used or interacted with by disparate groups, the boundary object works as a node connecting various social worlds of practice and experience. In other words, the boundary image/object enhances the capacity of an idea, concept, or theory to be intelligible across culturally or subculturally defined boundaries (Fox 2011). By this quality, the boundary image goes beyond representation and any textual/affective dualism by affording border crossing and thereby the connectivity of a network where human and nonhuman histories and entities are equally involved. This traversing capacity can often be a good thing; boundary objects and images are a necessary feature of any diversified cultural and interpersonal exchange of sensibilities made in pursuit of a progressive contemporary society. However, social systems of power shaped by networks of capital, whiteness, authoritarian regimes, and neoliberal governance prioritize certain exchanges and border crossings over others. In this context, calls for multiculturalism become requirements for participation in white, nuclear family or nationalist molds (Puar 2007).

Examples of this process are deeply varied and can showcase the elusiveness of boundary objects as well as their function as a mechanism of cultural sameness and everyday white supremacy, as seen through algorithmic racisms (Buolamwini 2017; Noble 2018) that structure computer-vision models as discussed in chapter 3. Nevertheless, "digital supremacy" has a long history. In an article published in the 1990s on racial passing online, Lisa Nakamura (1995) describes how technological affordances of the text-based massively multiplayer online role-playing game LambdaMOO facilitate a socially policed boundary crossing between racialized identities, where crossing into a stereotyped image of nonmodern Asianness is what the community authenticates as acceptable play. On this text-based game platform, users can only describe their in-world characters with words. Despite the supposed endless possibilities of the platform to describe one's body, Nakamura points out that when users describe themselves as African American, as Asian American or Latino, other users respond with hostility. These markers of nonwhite identity are seen as inherently antagonistic, as politicizing an otherwise a "neutral" space. Descriptions of nonwhiteness are allowed, however, when they ascribe to stereotyped versions of south or east Asian racial stereotypes. Users often described their characters as young submissive Asian women, or fantasy versions of the samurai. Nakamura (1995) describes this as identity tourism, where whiteness seeks to pass as the colonized other by donning those features of nonwhiteness set by orientalist narratives (Said 1978). Nakamura relates this to Edward Said's (1978) discussion of tourism and colonial fiction, where the imperialist adventurer experiences the pleasures and thrills of cross-cultural performance while simultaneously maintaining power over how otherness is defined and allowed to exist. The digital space of the game world, like the physical colonized state, presents a space where boundary crossing via identity tourism serves relations of power.

The boundary crossing done here is made possible through the textual invocation of a racialized image, afforded by a platform feature. The textually presented image of the stereotyped, orientalized other is thus a boundary image that affords "passing" from whiteness into foreignness defined by whiteness, thereby reproducing the dominance of these racialized narratives within the game-world. Apart from the boundary images however, identity tourism is also facilitated through the mainstream sociality of the online world it emerges from, where whiteness is default and nonracialized, and where expressions of nonwhiteness are policed in subconscious ways by users to maintain the default settings. In this example, it is not sufficient to attempt to identify a single boundary object or image, nor to limit the concept of image to a static visual presentation. Rather, the "crossing" of identity tourism emphasizes the need to conceptualize images as representations that function as vibrant nodes continuously concocted via their relations with colonial or imperial histories and institutions of contemporary power. Here, the coexistence of actual, creative, and profound forms of difference are repressed by homophilic desires that are recursively spawned and made to feel natural via processes of performativity and homophilic networks, online and offline (Chun 2018; Devries 2022). In other words, such social and political systems of power—white supremacy, male supremacy, and the imperial state—shape how and what the public prefers to interact with and the subsequent boundary mechanisms that emerge. Boundary images, unsurprisingly, are often representative of these homophilic states. In turn, boundary images are involved in how people come to believe in things like nationalist and/or biological truths. These processes involving boundary images are an essential part of what these chapters investigate.

Importantly, by nature of its affordances for crossing, the concept of boundary image also highlights the need to develop border consciousness throughout life and scholarship (Anzaldúa 1991). If borderlands are places where different nations, notions, or ontologies touch each other, what kind of border consciousness is necessary to "see" images that are hybrid and networked and increasingly "visible" to machines as data models? As mentioned, the border consciousness that we develop with boundary images moves our attention from the centre to the edges of the image, and then further beyond toward their systematically produced social and material infrastructures, histories, and ideologies. However, at the same time that these virtual crossings via boundary images contribute to "silent" mechanisms of social power, we must also acknowledge the very physical and similarly racialized violence of borders elsewhere. While we are working with nonhuman entities (boundary images and their networks), amid this work is violence imposed on humans via borders and regimes, especially upon those people that are often excluded from who counts as a human. When Gloria Anzaldúa writes about the U.S.–Mexico border, she calls it "una herida abierta" [an open wound] where the Global South "grates against the [imperialist world] and bleeds" (Anzaldúa 1991, 3). She proposes "mestiza" as a "new mythos" that creates border consciousness and as a way to theorize differences in the context of the Chicana community, their migration routes, and their experiences as Latino migrants in Americas. As we are writing this, borders are sites of violence also at all ends of fortress Europe, most notably the southern and eastern borders marked by the Mediterranean sea and by ancient forests, respectively.

These are highly patrolled areas, guarded in a nationalist spirit of "protection," familiarly defending the continent from illegal crossings. When apprehended at these sites of crossing, migrants are moved to prison-like detention centers and refugee camps, or are pushed back across the Polish–Belorussian border and left to live in the woods without access to food, water, or medical care. Among them are those who do not survive these attempted crossings; their bodies washed onto the beach or found in the forest. More than fifty-one thousand migrants have been reported dead or missing globally since 2014. By no coincidence, at the same time the United States has ramped up their border control and border violence. Importantly, alleged protection of the homeland from those characterized and treated as subhuman others via borders is in no way a new or 'extremist' practice, rather it is an outcome of imperialist statehood (McVeigh & Estrep 2019). The crossings made despite these harsh and nationalist policings, attempts in pursuit

of life and promise, are obviously not metaphorical nor theoretical
but struggles of humanity.

While our chapters do not address the migration crisis in Europe,
North America, and elsewhere, they address the work and affects
that boundary images have within far-right and fascist ontologies,
authoritarian regimes, and other sites of post- or pre-violent
crossings. Each of the articles approaches boundary images as part
of the continuous constitution of oppressive political and societal
contexts. If we are to fulfil the push to consider images beyond
representation in our methods and research projects, we must also
consider images as operating within a field of political tensions that
are situated in a much wider socio-technological infrastructure—
hence their qualification as boundary images. "Boundary images"
are both beyond representation and also beyond the metaphorical
category that the concept of "boundary image" might invoke.
They are instead a particular kind of image that always carries
political weight in its networked re-presentation and facilitation of
homophilic and thus often hierarchical, racializing ways of being. At
the same time, they are also openings onto multiple subjects and
subjectivities that make those borders. In analyzing how images
are caught up in processes of boundary making, inevitably political
struggle is a shared and central concern in this book. In doing so,
we find our chapters align with the question asked by Bennett
(2010, viii): "how do political responses to public problems change
when we take seriously the vitality of (nonhuman) bodies."

In this sense, the study of boundary images highlights often
otherwise bypassed social and oppressive infrastructures and the
processes that build them. In chapter 1, we encounter infrastructures that legitimize a network of censoring platforms. Chapter 2,
on the other hand, investigates infrastructures of belief that formulate embodied realities that oppose the pursuits for social science
and democracy. In chapter 3, machine-learning algorithms provide
both patterned and divergent infrastructures. While allowing focus
on the work boundary images do as and within various infrastructures, the concept of boundary image also allows us to study how

image boundaries are contested and negotiated via human and automated labors that involve various human–computer interactions, since an image's capacity to function as boundary image in part depends on its ability to be taken up by multiple actors or institutions within a network.

The new politics of the image that we evoke here refers to inextricable struggles at various scales, from state and corporate control of the citizen's gaze to the spread of conspiracy and far-right politics (Crary 2022). Images today occupy communication, affective relationships, infrastructure, and bodies via scanning systems, censoring algorithms, and various applications. Therefore, when we discuss the politics of the image in this book, we are speaking not only of the associations between politics and image but of its conversion into one of the main fields of current tensions and disputes, where powers, becomings, narratives, and resistances intersect. Although these three chapters are situated within specific political contexts and struggles, separated by international as well as ontological borders, our shared aim is to focus on how images are both politically produced and also involved in political problems by revealing some of the traces, logics, and parameters of their socio-technological infrastructure. Each chapter offers a unique method of tracing and doing image analysis, in which the digital, material, symbolic, and political come together to generate the life and opacity of each image.

Borders and Crossings

In this sense, images live because they generate relations and because, even if incidentally, images are affective and thus forceful in commanding the environments they occupy. Familiar examples of such environments used to be churches and museums, followed closely by books and maps. While churches and museums are spaces of worship and ritual in part constructed via icons and imagery, books and maps are artifacts that house images and present worlds. In the three chapters, images occupy computational, networked, (inter)national, and (super)natural environments, and are thus studied as part of ecologies where various entities are caught up in relations and frictions that take time. These relational ecologies that stretch across time and locations sustain the political dimensions and the lives of images.

The result of this linkage between the images we write about and also between us as new working colleagues is a book that reflects generational, national, historic, and personal differences of field and positionality. Our authorial differences are unique products of cultural, temporal, spatial, and academic boundaries. By leaving these diversities unsmoothed and unresolved in accordance with our resistance to the canonical nature of "boundary" and stable ontologies, we hope for *Boundary Images* to embody the capacity for a given academic concept to be useful in settings not bound by disciplinary expectations, allowing readers to benefit as we did from hearing from each other. In accordance with such interdisciplinary projects, the precise definition and use of "boundary image" varies within each chapter. At the same time, as hopefully made clear by the discussion above, *Boundary Images* is unified by our shared interest in the investigation of the capacities and politics of images to constitute and transcend the different borders that operate at various moments within human experience and organization. And as our different examples of working with boundary image as an analytical tool are evident in each of the chapters, having "border consciousness" is helpful in attuning ourselves to the strangely similar peripheries that these images occupy. In what follows, we give a brief discussion of each chapter, mentioning how each uses the concept of boundary images. We hope that this preview serves as a helpful guide for readers coming from digital media studies, studies of visual culture, or digital ethnography, as well as interdisciplinary scholars hoping to learn from the unfamiliar.

Chapter 1, "Cartographies of *Unerasable Images,*" considers internet images as those that are generated and distributed through networked computational processes. This distinction points beyond image circulation and distribution over networks to the generative act where images are created with technologies, such as through image transfer protocol (ITP) and image compression algorithms, at the moment when they appear on the computer screen, delivered via the internet. Not only do such technologies occupy space but they also generate new spatial forms that are situated, social, necessarily political, technological, and aesthetic. While always ready to be retrieved, the millions of images that are stored and mirrored on internet servers do not always end up visible to users. Subsequently, this chapter shows how availability and visibility of images are two different concepts. They are a combination of human and nonhuman forces distributed across virtual and physical locations that, while making images visible or not, renders them geopolitically as censored and algorithmically distributed.

Chapter 1 asks: How can we see internet images as carrying the residue of computational, social, and political conditions of their making? Answering this, the authors, the artist and curator, read one artwork together and argue that in order to see internet images for what they are, these images need to be read as map artifacts: abstractions of data rather than visual representations of things and symbols that stand in for subjects. Once located within networked infrastructures that are material, social, political, and geographical, the boundary of the images' circulation becomes highly volatile, especially as it is conditioned by networked protocols and computational technologies. "Legitimate boundary" alludes to the vagueness, uncertainties, and constant shifting of (hidden) rules in which something can be made illegitimate or prohibited for only a short time, especially in the context of digital and other forms of authoritarianism. In the end, this analysis shows how internet images are always part of relations that render them (in)visible. Cyberspace, the environment in which internet images circulate, keeps urgent the question about what images are, since the boundaries between different kinds of images are drawn and redrawn continuously. Boundaries are many and they are always

negotiated, even if they have been in place for a very long time.
How we see or define an image or its boundaries then depends on techniques used for its making and the rules and codes (legal and technical) that govern images' appearance in the world.

The second chapter, "Real-Making with Boundary Images: Ethnographic Explorations of Far-Right Worlds," deals more with boundary crossing than boundaries themselves as a way to interrogate new renditions of old racisms and conspiracy. More specifically, this chapter presents an anthropological approach informed by the author's personal and ethnographically cultivated positionality to understand how digital and nondigital images make conspiratorial or far-right worldviews compellingly real to adherents, despite a lack of physical evidence for the tangible existence of such worlds. Very often, studies of far-right subjectivities emphasize the concept of bounded group identity and distinction-making from an abject other as a critical feature of fascist ideology. As Jason Stanley (2020, 187) writes in *How Fascism Works,* "Fascist politics traffic in delusions that create these kinds of false distinctions between us and them, regardless of obvious realities." In turn, far-right adherents are often imagined as folks siphoned off from the mainstream and from observable, objective reality. Boundary-keeping is positioned as a common practice of far-right adherents, but this chapter's contextual foray posits whether the far-right "political other" is more enmeshed with mainstream institutions and belief practice than we would like to think.

It is certainly true that far-right ideology functions (often inconsistently) through distinct boundary and border maintenance, venerating supremacist hierarchies that sharply mark the "worthy" from the "unworthy," the "strong" from the "weak," the "welcome" from the "unwelcome," and the "pure" from the "polluted." However, this chapter shows how such boundaries are hard to manage on a daily basis. Contrary to our stereotypical assumptions about the stubbornness of the conspiratorial right, this chapter proposes that these are far from stable realities for adherents, and that they require constant upkeep and re-doing in order to remain compelling. To depict these processes of maintenance, chapter 2 conceptualizes boundary images not as image-objects that write boundaries between "us and them" through their rhetoric or symbolisms, but instead as infrastructures that materialize belief and enable recurrent crossings from one experiential reality (everyday normative life) into another, alternative world, where conspiratorial monsters and threats possess an imminent presence that is felt in an embodied way. In this sense, chapter 2 works to understand how images are involved in the cultivation of compelling, conspiratorial, yet embodied conceptions of the world that gain their felt-realness via users' continued interaction with vibrant images that allow contact with the features of this alternative world. It is in the moments where we come to interact with such worlds through material images that seemingly "unbelievable" worlds, monsters, or heroes become a bit more real and tangible, thus cultivating political conviction (Harding 1987).

Importantly, the brief historical discussions in chapter 2 push against the concept of a solid boundary between the mainstream and contemporary far-right conspiracy by emphasizing how a cultivated conviction in the unseen, the antiscientific, or the fundamentally unprovable is in fact a mainstream practice that has been normalized over time via powerful Christian and conservative institutions in the American and Canadian context. What this indicates is that the material practices and interactions that solidify the presence of invisible threats or heroic saviors are part of both fascist and mainstream life, as are the normalized logics of white and male supremacy that afford the ease by which these images and the concepts they carry can be engaged.

The final chapter, "Galton Reloaded: Computer Vision and Machinic Eugenics," analyses political and aesthetic developments of computer vision and artificial intelligence, investigating the role of pattern conformation in its creation methodologies. It discusses computer vision as a dispositive shaping the contemporary gaze, pointing to its ideological and aesthetic unfoldings in social life. The text situates the ideological background of AI technologies in the context of anthropocentric thought, questioning the notions of intelligence, vision, learning, and neural networks conceptualized in its colonialist realm. Further, this chapter discusses the social production of data, particularly those datasets used in machine learning oriented to visual models. For that, the author highlights the racist, ageist, and misogynistic biases of artificial-intelligence architectures for synthesizing images. Among the synthetic images produced with computer-vision technologies, special attention is devoted to deepfakes and face-recognition analyses. Both are discussed as technocultural objects.

Concerning deepfakes, chapter 3 emphasizes the links between deepfakes and contemporary practices of historical denialism, and the unfolding of this in the memory of digital culture. Regarding computational techniques of facial analyses, the chapter highlights its connections with Francis Galton's Composite Portraits and his formulation of the "pictorial statistics." The chapter ponders how computer vision, and its pattern-based structure, updates the foundations of the eugenics imagination, focusing on ideological uses of biotechnologies, genetic algorithms, and transhumanism. Not less important in these discussions are the myriad of beautification apps used for the construction of ideal bodies, according to standards shaped by stereotypes and far-right mythologies. In tying these discussions together, chapter 3 argues that while the potential of artificial intelligence to shape fields of visibility will not imply genocidal racial wars, as the eugenic movements of the first half of twentieth century did, certain subjects and bodies will be algorithmically excluded from the social and political realm, intensifying socially produced opacities and new forms of invisibility. In its conclusion, it points to the need for deconstructing the potentials of an emergent machinic eugenics of the gaze by embracing counterhegemonic technological frameworks and images that fall outside the pattern.

On the most practical level, we dealt with the active effects of boundaries as coauthors separated from each other via borders drawn by governmental authorities and institutions, as each have

18   worked to manage space historically and global health contemporarily. As mostly strangers prior to this project (except for the authors of the first chapter, who have worked together for some time), each in different stages of our career, our chapters and we not only navigated different time zones and nationalities, but the limitations posed by the disparate but equally taxing demands of life and endless career building within the neoliberal academy, especially during the years of the Covid-19 pandemic. This meant that our evolving chapters came into contact with other projects, colleagues, obligations, anxieties, and even the virus itself for all four of us. In turn, *Boundary Images* cemented itself as a consistent presence in our work-from-homes and digitally mediated conversations with both colleagues and perhaps somewhat uninterested friends. Occasionally, despite blurry screens and audio issues, online video meetings brought us together. It was here within liminal digital spaces, across digital networks linking various living rooms and office spaces, with poorly pixelated faces complicated by background noises, that we began to understand how boundary images—both the book and the concept itself — would unfold. Through the bringing together of these diverse chapters, we have hoped to offer a wide set of examples in how we might use the concept of boundary image within the vast study of image ecologies. Further, having critiqued forms of bias, censorship, and reactionary systems of belief, we hope that future techniques will continue to recognize the inherent politics of boundary images as entities caught up in the networked maintenance of power. Let us continue to challenge and expand upon our growing knowledge of the networked lives, work, and boundaries of images.

References

Ahmed, Sara. 2008. "Imaginary Prohibitions: Some Preliminary Remarks on the Founding Gesture of 'New Materialism.'" *European Journal of Women's Studies* 15, no. 1:23–39.

Anzaldúa, Gloria. 1991. *Borderlands/La Frontera: The New Mestiza*. San Francisco: Aunt Lute Books.

Bennett, Jane. 2010. *Vibrant Matter: A Political Ecology of Things*. Durham, N.C.: Duke University Press.

Braidotti, Rosi. 2002. *Metamorphoses: Towards a Materialist Theory of Becoming*. Cambridge, UK: Polity.

Buolamwini, J. A. 2017. "Gender Shades: Intersectional Phenotypic and Demographic Evaluation of Face Datasets and Gender Classifiers." Masters thesis, Massachusetts Institute of Technology. https://dspace.mit.edu/bitstream/ handle/1721.1/114068/1026503582-MIT.pdf.

Chun, Wendy Hui Kyong. 2018. "Queerying Homophily." In *Pattern Discrimination*, ed. Clemens Apprich, Wendy Hui Kyong Chun, Florian Cramer, and Hito Steyerl, 59–98. Minneapolis: meson press and University of Minnesota Press.

Chun, Wendy Hui Kyong. 2008. "On 'Sourcery,' or Code as Fetish." *Configurations* 16, no. 3:299–324.

Crary, J. 2022. *Scorched Earth: Beyond the Digital Age to a Post-Capitalist World*. London: Verso.

Dewdney, A. and Sluis, K. eds. 2022. *The Networked Image in Post-Digital Culture*. Taylor & Francis.

Devries, M. 2022. "Archetypes and Homophilic Avatars: New Approaches to Studying Far-Right Facebook Practice." *Canadian Journal of Communication* 47, no. 1:151–71.

Fox, Nick J. 2011. "Boundary Objects, Social Meanings, and the Success of New Technologies." *Sociology* 45, no. 1: 70–85. https://doi.org/10.1177/0038038510387196.

Harding, Susan. 1991. "Representing Fundamentalism: The Problem of the Repugnant Cultural Other." *Social Research* 58, no. 2: 373–93.

Harding, Susan F. 1987. "Convicted by the Holy Spirit: The Rhetoric of Fundamental Baptist Conversion." *American Ethnologist* 14, no. 1: 167–81.

Hemmings, Clare. 2005. "Invoking Affect: Cultural Theory and the Ontological Turn." *Cultural Studies* 19, no. 5: 548–67.

Hughes, Brian. 2019. "Thriving from Exile: Toward a Materialist Analysis of the Alt-Right." *boundary 2*, September 24.

Lennon, Myles. 2018. "Revisiting 'The Repugnant Other' in the Era of Trump." *HAU: Journal of Ethnographic Theory* 8, no. 3: 439–54. https://doi.org/10.1086/700979.

McVeigh, Rory, and Kevin Estep. 2019. *The Politics of Losing: Trump, the Klan, and the Mainstreaming of Resentment*. New York: Columbia University Press.

Mitchell, W. J. T. 2005. *What Do Pictures Want? The Lives and Loves of Images*. Chicago: University of Chicago Press.

Noble, S. U. 2018. *Algorithms of Oppression: How Search Engines Reinforce Racism*. New York: New York University Press.

Paasonen, Susanna. 2011. "Introduction: Carnal Appeal." In *Carnal Resonance: Affect and Online Pornography*, 1–29. Cambridge, Mass.: MIT Press.

Parikka, Jussi, and Tony Sampson. 2009. "On Anomalous Objects of Digital Culture." In *The Spam Book: On Viruses, Porn, and Other Anomalies from the Dark Side of Digital Culture*, ed. Jussi Parikka and Tony Sampson, 1–18. Cresskill, N.J.: Hampton Press.

Pasquinelli, M., and Joler, V. 2020. "The Nooscope Manifested: Artificial Intelligence as

20 Instrument of Knowledge Extractivism." KIM research group (Karlsruhe University of Arts and Design) and Share Lab (Novi Sad). https://nooscope.ai.

Puar, Jasbir K. 2007. *Terrorist Assemblages: Homonationalism in Queer Times.* Durham, N.C.: Duke University Press.

Said, Edward W. 1978. *Orientalism.* London: Routledge.

Star, Susan Leigh. 2010. "This Is Not a Boundary Object: Reflections on the Origin of a Concept." *Science, Technology, & Human Values* 35, no. 5: 601–17. https://doi.org/10.1177/0162243910377624.

Star, Susan Leigh, and James R. Griesemer. 1989. "Institutional Ecology, 'Translations,' and Boundary Objects: Amateurs and Professionals in Berkeley's Museum of Vertebrate Zoology, 1907–39." *Social Studies of Science* 19, no. 3: 387–420. https://doi.org/10.1177/030631289019003001.

Venturini, T. 2021. "Toward a Sociology of Online Monsters: Online Conspiracy Theories and the Secondary Orality of Digital Platforms." https://hal.science/hal-03464174.

1

Cartographies of *Unerasable Images*

Winnie Soon and Magdalena Tyżlik-Carver

> In its most extended sense, then, a picture refers to the entire situation in which an image has made its appearance, as when we ask someone if they "get the picture."
>
> —W. J. T. Mitchell

In this chapter we ask what the image is and how one gets to see it, to paraphrase Mitchell, when the image and the terrain where it appears are computationally executed, highly networked, and dynamically generated. The computer screen frames the site on which computer-generated images appear. It is the meeting point of the physical, digital, and symbolic channeled algorithmically as input and output, and it renders data into perceivable forms, such as images and texts, to the user. All images need a display if they are to be visible. While the computer screens are locations for digital images to appear, they also afford human–computer interactions (Allen 2016; Tyżlik-Carver 2022). As such, what we see via the screen is not just an image but always already a result of mediated processes and interactions that involve others and not just humans. Such a moment of image generation and display is what we focus on in this chapter, with a specific attention to internet images.

Our interest is in internet images and how to see them, and we argue that they are locations that carry the residue of the computational, social, and political conditions of their making. To account for these conditions contained in and by the image, we propose to read internet images as maps. Traditionally, a map defines the terrain and its borders by symbolically representing and locating its features on a surface. A map is not an objective representation but an interpretation and abstraction of physical elements that can be found in the world and captured in the form of a map. An internet image can be seen as a map, too, where data is abstracted and processed to represent things and subjects. However, what we are interested in seeing in the internet image are not the things it represents but bodies of data, their flows and relations that make images appear or disappear online. While internet images might refer to any image that circulates on the internet and its many platforms, we define internet images as those that are generated and distributed through networked computational processes such as image transfer protocol (ITP) and image compression algorithms. The distinction points beyond circulation and distribution, to the generative act where images are created through the computational and networked processing and delivered not only via the internet. At the same time, while internet images result from algorithmic and data processing, and human–computer interactions, we propose that the internet images, such as those that appear in image search results, represent geopolitical and algorithmic as well as subjective forces that compete to make pictures available on the internet. These forces include algorithmic conditions resulting from combinations of search words, indexing algorithms, classification and metadata systems, as well as political and social conditions where what is visible corresponds, though not directly, to one's geographic location in the internet network. The millions of images that are stored and mirrored on the internet servers, while always ready to be retrieved, do not always end up visible to users. Avail-

[Figure 1.1]. A zoom-in frame of the Lego Tank Man in *Unerasable Images*, 2017. Copyright Winnie Soon 2017.

ability and visibility are two different concepts, and searching for an image does not ensure it will appear in the search results. For example, it is common knowledge that politically sensitive images are not visible on the Chinese internet, where the technological and political come together to render what is (in)visible. In such a situation the human engagement can be seen simultaneously as incidental (because the result always excludes restricted content) and infrastructural (because through censorship it shapes what is excluded). It is the combination of these human and nonhuman forces distributed across virtual and physical locations that, while making images visible or not, renders them geopolitically so they can be read as a map.

Looking closely at situations in which images (dis)appear on the internet, we map what cannot be seen directly in the image but what is infrastructurally part of it. To do this we use Winnie Soon's artwork *Unerasable Images* (2017) to think about highly networked characteristics of computationally generated images. *Unerasable Images* is a durational work developed over the course of one year by the artist's daily interactions with the internet through a web browser and Google Search engine. To make this artwork, the artist searches for an image that is a Lego reconstruction of the so-called Tank Man (see Figure 1.1), a highly censored photograph from 1989 demonstration on Tiananmen Square in Beijing, depicting a peaceful demonstrator with bags in each hand, facing a string of advancing military tanks. Normally such a photograph, because of the subject it depicts, would be immediately removed. In this case, however, the Lego Tank Man was only removed after a few hours since it was first published on the Chinese web portal 网易 on the May 31, 2013, after enough time for servers worldwide to copy and distribute it so that it now appears occasionally in search results outside of China. Screenshots, once collected, are manipulated by the artist who deletes all images displayed on the first page of the search results, leaving only the image of the Lego Tank Man. The work *Unerasable Images* animates the movement of this thumbnail image across the screen. This movement represents the computational sorting that arranges images on the page and on the screen. With the disappearance and appearance through censorship in China and Google searching available in the rest of the world, the Lego Tank Man image sets the spatial and legitimate boundary between domestic (within China) and foreign (outside of China) arenas. Geographic borders of Chinese territory become boundaries within which the image of the Lego Tank Man may not appear. And they also point to ambiguities generated by interactions across online and offline spaces, which are vaguely endorsed or opposed by Chinese authorities. We use the term *legitimate spaces* to discuss how an image is made (in)visible through the complexity of governance, history, humans, and machines. The work *Unerasable Images* marks the boundaries of the Lego Tank Man image perceivable as the work becomes a legitimate space for the image to exist.

We trace *Unerasable Images* as a boundary image that frames the terrain on which internet images appear and disappear. We read *Unerasable Images,* as a map, a cartographic representation of algorithmic relations that can be traced with(in) images. In this chapter, we discuss the specific image to show what (in)visible spaces are constructed and represented, and how technological and political come together to generate an image infrastructurally. Our aim here is to situate "where" the image is—that is, where and how it is created—and we locate it within computational and networked infrastructures. In this approach we want to account for the networked and computational locale of the internet that draws the boundary of images. Such mapping involves many complex data processes such as content filtering and personalization (Deibert 2008; Ridgway 2017), query operations (Jiang 2014; Snodgrass and Soon 2019; Soon and Cox 2020, 187–209), and web and image optimization (Rabbani and Jones 1991; Thylstrup and Teilmann 2017; Shehata 2019), among others. By tracing the networked processes that generate and reconstruct the image, and by mapping these processes on geographic territories that are governed by authorities, we propose that internet images are artifacts of internet infrastructures that make images (dis)appear online. Soon's work, *Unerasable Images,* represents what can be seen, and it captures what is not visible in the image.

Unerasable Images and the Tank Man (as Infrastructural Image)

Unerasable Images is a compilation of screenshots that maps infrastructures of internet image making, showing how the image appears in the web browser. While part of the artistic method, it reveals material constraints that are always present in sociotechnological networks with its complex dynamics and infrastructural compositions. For example, every time we see an image on the internet it is constructed for us almost on the spot, unless cached in the browser history. Image transport protocol (ITP) or picture transfer protocol (PTP) are some of the standards that deliver image data over networks, and they operate at the moment of accessing the picture. Images themselves are compressed into formats such as GIF (graphic interchange format) or JPEG (Joint

Photographic Expert Group image) to facilitate transport of data. Once the image starts to circulate on the internet, it is copied and reproduced endlessly and merges with processes of image construction so that in the end it appears on the screen. On the internet, situations of making an image always involve multiple computational processes taking place at different levels of data processing executed at different times.

Processes of data manipulation, while technologically framed, include social and political constraints, and *Unerasable Images* attempts to map those too. There is a certain dynamic present within the systems, which allows objects to evolve "in relation to discrete environments," which are "at once physical, political, and social and that take in legal and religious domains as well as the internal, technical logic of machines" (Larkin 2018, 197). In such discrete environments form results from human interventions and materiality of objects and things, and they cannot be separated. Indeed, there is material excess in technology, which is historical and discursive (Kittler 1992; 1999) and agential (Barad 2007). *Unerasable Images* works with this excess to capture infrastructural conditions of image making while using representational quality of a generated image as well as a response that such an image generates.

The process of searching for the Lego Tank Man, the image at the center of *Unerasable Images,* took place almost every day of 2017, resulting in a collection of more than three hundred screenshots of a browser window with the search results page. The query given to the search engine, was always the same: "六四" ("64"), a reference to June 4, the month and the day of the crackdown on the student-led Tiananmen Square Protest in Beijing in 1989, and it would always deliver a selection of thumbnail images organized into a grid on the pages of Google search results. The aim of the daily search was to look for the photograph depicting the Lego reconstruction of another photograph famously taken in 1989 and titled "The Tank Man stopping the column of T59 tanks." The Lego version of this scene was reconstructed, photographed, and published in 2013 on the Chinese web portal. Screenshots, once collected, are manipulated by the artist who erases all thumbnails from the original page, except for the one image of the Lego Tank Man. What remains are pictures of a white web page, at times completely empty and at other times with one or two thumbnail images in it. The usual grid that organizes the resulting images on the page is erased and the only visible content is the one image that moves across the browser page with each screenshot (see Figure 1.1). In the browser tab, two Chinese characters can be read, together with a URL with complex parameters and the Google Image Search page with the Google logo in the left upper corner. *Unerasable Images* is based on a process of screenshooting[1] that emphasizes the act of capturing what is visible on the computer screen to collect evidence of memory of an event reconstructed as a Lego installation. And while the work traces the image, it makes visible how censorship is executed on the internet.

The image of the Tank Man is widely known in the world as a symbol of the events at Tiananmen Square in June 1989. The Tank Man, like many other photographs from that time, is censored in China. Indeed, anything related to the Tiananmen Square protests and massacre, such as the words *June* and *Fourth*, numeric characters *198964,* related interviews and images, are politically sensitive content. Censorship has been applied not only to the historical photographs but to any kind of use and reappropriation of symbols that might provoke and produce collective memory. In effect it is impossible to search for, share, or see these images within China. The appearance of the Lego reproduction of the Tank Man intervenes into this status quo as the image became visible on the Chinese internet for a short time in 2013, ahead of the twenty-fourth anniversary of the event, proving that the memory of the event is still alive.

Although there were many photographers and journalists who witnessed and captured the events in the center of Beijing in 1989, it is the scene represented in the figure of the Tank Man that has become the symbol of the tragic events. The image was taken on the fifth of June, around noon, the day after Tiananmen Square had been cleared by the Chinese army. Stewart Franklin, one of the photographers of the Tank Man, describes the situation:

> A group of civilians lined up to face a double row of sol-
> diers who themselves stood in firing positions in front of
> a column of tanks. These civilians were shot at repeatedly,
> leaving at least twenty casualties. As the bodies were
> carried away the standoff died down and a column of
> tanks broke through, moving slowly eastwards. Waiting
> for them a few hundred metres down the road was a man
> in a white shirt and dark trousers, carrying two shopping
> bags. Alone he blocked the path of the tanks, watched by
> groups of nervous bystanders and perhaps fifty journal-
> ists, camera crews and photographers on balconies on
> almost every floor of the hotel. (Franklin 2016)

Franklin, Jeff Widener, Charlie Cole, and Hong Kong photographer Arthur Tsang all captured this scene in powerful images that to this day represent the violence of the events and the powerlessness of the people against the tanks and armaments of the China Libera-tion Army that killed and wounded thousands of protesters.[2] While the four photographs differ in minor details, and Cole's and Tsang's photographs are less often cited, they all captured this moment of a struggle embodied in the Tank Man as an icon of the events. Widely distributed and published in the West, the photograph remains "an icon of public memory" (Casey 2004, 20) and an image that "transcends the monumental space of Tiananmen, reifying him [the Tank Man] as a cultural symbol of resistance endlessly circulated and consumed without context yet a mnemonic memory of Western media in accessing China" (Ibrahim 2016, 587). Yasmin Ibrahim refers to this as "iconic new production," which collapses "complex events into media imagery" (587) where the image becomes a memory of an event while abstracting its historical situatedness and replacing it with the Tank Man as "an unfinis-hed narrative" and "enigmatic entity" (586). The scene has been reappropriated globally and countlessly in the form of memes, cartoons, posters, desktop images, graffiti, performances, and many other expressions (Andaluz 2012; Hills 2014; Coconuts Hong Kong 2018), and as such it encapsulates what Ibrahim describes as "global spectacle" (2016, 586). Ibrahim's critique shows how media imagery become news icons, and in the process their historical and political power, which might obliterate "what came before and what may come after" (588), collapses. At the same time, she recognizes circulation of such imagery on the internet as a form of social collective memory, where repressed and censored events find ways to be commemorated via digital technology, networked circulation, and social media.

The artwork *Unerasable Images* also makes use of the Tank Man's iconic status, but it does so to redefine image as data and to query the complex relations between censorship and image circulation on the internet. By reproducing the Lego Tank Man with the more than three hundred screenshots used for making *Unerasable Images,* the work proves that the image circulates on the internet in some uncontrollable manner, while it is always ready to be called by the keyword search. Soon's work traces technological, geographical, political, and social conditions for collective memory on social media and within certain borders and territories. While in the West the Tank Man is the news icon worthy of being published on the front pages of newspapers and to freely circulate online, in China this image, along with many others, is highly censored and never to be seen in public. The Lego reproduction of the Tank Man makes the image harder for bots and humans who censor the Chinese internet to recognize it, giving the image time to become data circulating over networks. Such data, once copied and distributed by servers, is hard to delete and erase. *Unerasable Images* captures daily appearances of the Lego Tank Man as it continues to circulate worldwide in a paradoxical gesture of countercensorship. The central framing of the Lego Tank Man in *Unerasable Images* as the only image on Google search results page becomes a memorial of the events of 1989 and evidence of infrastructural conditions that control visibility of this image.

Internet: From Cyberspace to Infrastructure

We have known that, even after decentralization, control exists, inscribed as technological features distributed through internet protocols (Galloway 2004). Today, more than ever, the internet is a material topos infrastructurally organized through server farms, data centers, cables, and networks of computers that envelop the planet. But it is also a virtual space imagined, occupied, and continuously constructed with software and the ways in which it is produced and used. While internet images are computationally constructed as jpg files or similar, we consider them also as a residue of infrastructural conditions that include geographically distributed politics and sociality framed through technology. As scholars of software studies, who theorize digital culture and communication, as artist and curator, practitioners who produce and exhibit works of computational art and design that take into account different sensibilities to the materiality and aesthetics of data, our research into internet images focuses on how computational technologies and infrastructures become active in the production of art, culture, and widely understood sociality. And so, while control is technologically distributed, it can be also evidenced in images and how they are made visible or not by the internet infrastructures.

At the same time we recognize that artistic inventions and their material practices have generated images and representations of the virtual spaces of the internet, which complement and expand visualizations of internet networks. For example, if graphs, flowcharts, and similar technical formats are traditionally used to represent how information is distributed over networks (Shannon and Weaver 1998) or how data flows through a computer system (von Neumann 1945), artistic interventions help to create an image of otherwise conceptually distant environments in which networks, software, and data are seen to be the main occupants. In popular culture, William Gibson popularized the notion of cyberspace in his 1984 novel *Neuromancer*. The author introduced it already in his 1982 short story "Burning Chrome," in reference to a simulator, the

Cyberspace Seven, a piece of hardware built by Automatic Jack, one of the main characters of the story. However, the most prominent notion of cyberspace is that of "a matrix" regularly visited by Automatic Jack and his hacker friend Bobby Quinn, "an abstract representation of the relationship between data systems" (Gibson 1987, 169) This understanding of cyberspace is well explained in *Neuromancer* where its genealogy is traced to geometric shapes and their mathematical algorithms applied in computer graphics:

> "The matrix has its roots in primitive arcade games," said the voice-over, "in early graphics programs and military experimentation with cranial jacks." On the Sony, a two-dimensional space war faded behind a forest of mathematically generated ferns, demonstrating the spatial possibilities of logarithmic spirals; cold blue military footage burned through, lab animals wired into test systems, helmets feeding into fire control circuits of tanks and war planes. "Cyberspace. A consensual hallucination experienced daily by billions of legitimate operators, in every nation, by children being taught mathematical concepts . . . A graphic representation of data abstracted from the banks of every computer in the human system. Unthinkable complexity. Lines of light ranged in the nonspace of the mind, clusters and constellations of data. Like city lights, receding . . ." (Gibson 1984, 51)

The relation between the graphics of arcade games and the imagined space constructed purely as an abstraction of what is otherwise a "nonspace of mind" frames the vision of cyberspace in the novel, and it is also a conceptual model for how the notion of digital space has been referenced and imagined in popular culture ever since. The complexity of cyberspace is surely unthinkable, inasmuch as it is both a concrete network and an imaginary space of vast nodes, and in "Burning Chrome" it is abstracted into a cyberpunk aesthetic of a dark and dystopian vision of the world and the paranoid relations that govern it.

However, there is an earlier and different version of cyberspace. In their essay written on the occasion of the 2015 exhibition *What's Happening?* at Statens Museum for Kunst in Copenhagen, Jacob Lillemose and Mathias Kryger (2015) remind us of the vision of cyberspace imagined and created by the Danish artist Susanne Ussing and architect Carsten Hoff. The artistic duo, also known as Atelier Cyberspace, between 1968 and 1970 generated the body of work dedicated to cyberspace. Their vision of the cyberspace is realized as architectural installations and visual collages that imagine and produce cyberspace without using a computer. For the artists, inspired by cybernetics and science and art collaborations, "'cyberspace' was simply about managing spaces" that were concrete and physical (Hoff in Lillemose and Kryger 2015). Unlike Gibson's dystopian vision of cyberspace, Ussing's collages depict it as a curious location housing organic and geometrical shapes with human figures among them. Physical installations by Atelier Cyberspace were experimental prototypes that were intended to intervene into the "rigid confines of urban planning" (Hoff in Lillemose and Kryger 2015), creating material and sensorial experience of the cyberspace rather than its ephemeral version with little to no space for the body to enter. These studies trace and propose social patterns that are part of cybernetic environments as explorative networks where relations emerge and are created through interactions between human and nonhuman bodies that inhabit these cyberspaces. This is a different vision of cyberspace than that offered in *Neuromancer*. However, rather than a utopian study, it is an experiment in building environments that create conditions for architecturally constructed networks to experiment with.

The work of Atelier Cyberspace suggests that the physical experience of cyberspace is important. But as cyberspace stands for a virtual space where the abstraction of computational conditions is experienced through various forms of the internet use, such as computer games or social media, we are reminded that "where technology is located is as important as *what* it is" (Deibert 2015, 10; original emphasis). The question of how software matters in the world has been asked by software studies scholars, who for some time recognized that "software structures and makes possible much of the contemporary world" (Fuller 2008, 1) and that network technologies are "essentially control technologies" (Chun 2008, 1). Today, when computation sustains functions on which societies depend, processes of digitalization illustrate how this tendency continuously expands, and software as part of digital infrastructures transforms "all social and organizational levels" (Edwards et al. 2009). Similarly, the digital turn has been widely discussed in geography (Ash, Kitchin, and Leszczynski 2018; Burns 2021). From the impact of GIS (geographic information systems) technologies on capture, analysis, and visualization of space (Sui 2004), to the mapping of changing geographies of global trade in electronic waste (Lepawsky 2015), and the distribution of data centers across the world and their ecologies (Hogan 2018), the effect of digital technologies in the geographic field also affects geographic distribution of different stages of computational production and the production of computers. These spatial formations are the result of software and its workings in the world. As Robert Kitchin and Martin Dodge argue, "code is a product of the world and [. . .] code does work in the world" (2011, 16). Importantly, what is also being produced in the process of global distribution of computing and computation is a notion of space as new "spacialities of everyday life and new modes of governance and creativity (which are themselves inherently spatial)" (Kitchin and Dodge 2011, 16). Not only do such technologies occupy space but they also generate new spatial forms that are situated, social (that is, political), technological, and aesthetic.

Internet activities look simple—getting online and exchanging data, but "they are in fact embedded in a complex infrastructure (material, logistical, and regulatory) that in many cases crosses several borders" (Kitchin and Dodge 2011, 16). In China, the state uses technologies to censor internet information and to block access to selected foreign websites and content as part of what is usually called the Great Firewall of China (The Golden Shield

Project), initiated by the Ministry of Public Security division of the Chinese government. The internet is considered in the framework of "Internet sovereignty" (Wang 2014; Zeng, Stevens, and Chen 2017), according to which the country has the right to control and regulate its domestic cyberspace. Clearly, cyberspace is not a universal terrain. According to the white paper in 2010, the Chinese cyberspace belongs to the Chinese territory, a space concerning "national economic prosperity and development, state security and social harmony, state sovereignty and dignity" that needs to be administered because "within Chinese territory the Internet is under the jurisdiction of Chinese sovereignty" (People's Daily Online 2010). Under these conditions, infrastructural and geopolitical borders are superimposed in Chinese internet, and censorship serves to prevent "China's domestic cyberspace from being merged with foreign cyberspaces" (Qiu 1999, 3). This extends the geopolitical control and governance for both "the tangible and intangible spaces" and it constructs the national level of the "China Wide Web" (Qiu 1999, 13). The experience of cyberspace in China is defined by high control of consumption, circulation, and production of content online, which, arguably, mirrors the conditions of living offline in the People's Republic of China. Not only do such technologies occupy space but they also generate new spatial forms that are situated, social (that is political), technological, and aesthetic. Indeed, Chinese censorship is a force that regulates the Chinese internet and as such it operates geopolitically. We focus on this aspect later in the chapter. Before that, we start with the image search as a technical and infrastructural function that conditions the experience of the internet as geopolitical.

Infrastructures of Image Search as (Geo)Politics of Search

Today cyberspace continues to be experienced through interactions via the internet. On the technical level, the internet frames a set of technical procedures that organizes and controls how data circulate. Among these procedures are those that determine if images can be erased from the internet completely or if they can be prevented from appearing in search results within the borders of a specific country. We refer to such operations as geopolitics of search—a situation of data censorship entangled with data management. Crawling, indexing, and ranking are the three major steps in the online search queries (Page, Brin, Motwani, and Winograd 1999; Jiang 2014, 2), and they refer to computational processes presented as search result pages of static images organized within a grid structure. In the framework of these queries, images are data to be processed, transmitted, and distributed across cyberspace. The availability and visibility of the Lego Tank Man image on the Google platform can be understood via this (geo)politics of search.

Crawling web pages is a computational technique that is used to scrape billions of websites worldwide and look for references to images.[3] Apart from crawling, Google Image Search also uses the technique of classification to analyze scraped and collected images. Classification is the process of identifying specified features of objects and putting them into categories. Classifying features organize objects into groups, such as photographs, images containing a face, images in color or black and white, and so on. Classification can also be based on object recognition, for instance differentiating between a tank, a man, and a plastic bag. Therefore, a specific image contains a variety of classifying features that are used to facilitate data organization, retrieval, and indexing. Similar classification techniques are common in the field of artificial intelligence, in which machines learn "to detect and interpret images" (Crawford and Paglen 2019). Many machine-learning processes are automated, yet automation is not purely technical but "inherently social and political" (Crawford and Paglen 2019). One of the reasons for this is that classification techniques involve defining discrete categories with decisions made at various stages of the process deciding on the names of categories and the labeling process. Crawling also involves many human decisions: for example, "which sites to crawl, how often, and how many pages to fetch from each site."[4] These are social and political processes as much as technical. From crawling to classifying techniques, every search image is extracted via automated processes to facilitate data organization. The process of image classification marks another boundary that defines the image by recognizing what is in it and thus indexing it for search algorithms.

Indexing is another technique of image search processing, where an image is associated with textual content (or keywords). The related textual content can be more than one label, and examples range from recognized object names that are predefined via classification techniques to the attributes and content tags from the associated web sites. Theoretically speaking, there could be many terms associated with the "same" image. For example, an image of a Lego Tank Man can be associated with "Tank Man," "Lego," "Toys," "June Fourth," "Cars," "Protest," "Art," "China," and so on. This associated textual content can come from object recognition, as well as keywords and other metadata from scraped websites. However, these related terms could be very broadly defined, which illustrates that indexing is a complicated process. Olga Goriunova describes this problem when she talks about formation of digital subjects that "arise out of computational procedures and are employed by various forms of power to distinguish, map, and capture not only subjectivities, but also non-humans and physical things that inhabit the world" (2019, 127). While this defines a process of "new computational subjectification" (127) it also illustrates the distance between a human being (as a subject) and its representation in terms of data profiling, in which "data and subject are indexically and repeatedly linked" (Raley in Goriunova 2019, 132). In the case of the Lego Tank Man, the image is associated with the keywords '6' and '4' (in Chinese characters), referring to a specific historical date, which in this case is also used to index the Lego Tank Man as a digital subject that can be retrieved (or not) with these two symbols. Indexing, when considered as computational subjectification, is dynamic in nature and highly dependent on algorithmic actions and interpretations.

Apart from crawling and indexing and their relations to data subjects, ranking provides "quality of search results" instead of "junk results" (Brin and Page 1998). This quality is computationally produced and spatially organized, which significantly influences our understanding of search terms/items/concepts because search engines relate to knowledge organization. As such, the search algorithm is a "culture machine" (Finn 2017, 89) that performs cultural works and presents knowledge to us via statistics and meaning creation. Ranking is one of the most powerful concepts in the modern web and platform culture inasmuch as it structures the order and determines the prioritization of visibility (Jiang 2014, 2). It is widely implemented in many search and e-commerce sites to present the most relevant listing. It is hierarchically and computationally organized to capture the prime attention of users to make them stay or to follow with actions, such as more clicking and buying. In business terms, ranking optimizes information to capture the attention of the user and to prompt further actions. Within ranking, sorting organizes items systematically in a sequence ordered by some predefined criterion. Sorting and arranging involve grouping and categorization with weighting criteria that are built into the algorithm. Ranking assigns values, prioritizing some images over others. In the context of an image search engine, prioritization ensures optimization; that is, relevance of search engine results is linked to the user's profile based on previous actions, behaviors, browsing histories, geographical locations, and preferences, among others (Zuboff 2015; Noble 2018; Ridgway 2021). Consequently, the prioritization in ranking is not the same for every user but dynamic in nature—a query is executed and the result is generated on the fly for every ranking list/page. As such, ranking of data is generated in real-time through computational and dynamic processes, impacting which images are made (in)visible, to whom, and where.

How the Lego Tank Man image appears in the work of *Unerasable Images* reflects classification, indexing, and ranking executed in the background by search engines. It was only in 2016 that the image of the Lego Tank Man caught the attention of the artist

[Figure 1.2]. Nine selected images in *Unerasable Images*, 2018. Copyright Winnie Soon.

when browsing the internet while at home in Denmark (see Figure 1.2). Outside China, Google Search does not have to comply with Chinese regulations to censor inappropriate content, even if it was uploaded within the Chinese territory. The search result images that appear as thumbnails—smaller in size and compressed—are stored in a database so they are ready to be retrieved at any point. There is an indexical relation, which is digitized, traceable, and computable, between the keyword and the image. To compute it, Google algorithms work with browsing histories, personalized preferences, geographic locations and IP addresses, the value of words (Thornton 2017; 2018), indexed keywords, and other unknown parameters and weight factors (Bifet et al. 2005; Jing and Baluja 2008; Wang et al. 2011). More importantly, what is displayed on the image search reflects Google's priorities and profiling of users, resulting in the presentation of relevant content. Unlike the need to comply with the censoring rules of an authoritarian state, profiling users supports content optimization for profit-making under the logic of neoliberalism that aims to extract value from all internet activities.

It is at this point that the artist intervenes into the process of value extraction by performing a year-long screenshooting of the image search results. The production of the artwork *Unerasable Images* utilizes the same keywords search to capture the first result page daily. Each stored image has a volatile computed value that governs each image's rank in which different cues make up the rules of search algorithm to prioritize the vast amount of images in databases. The Lego Tank Man sometimes appears on the first page, and other times it does not, resulting in an empty browser window. In this artwork, the Lego Tank Man is the only visible thumbnail that occupies a small cell from a larger grid system, which is a fundamental structure that organizes multiple images in an orderly and spatial manner. Thumbnails, with their compressed format and reduced file size, are infrastructural images (Thylstrup and Teilmann 2017), which, like in the case of poor images, facilitate "the flow and exchange of images" (2017, 285). These infrastructural thumbnail images have an "indexical role," enabling a much faster and efficient information retrieval and further point to other links of the world (2017, 281). To compute a grid system on the image search interface requires a list of indexical arrays to cycle through each row and each column. Each individual thumbnail image with the same height can be placed at the right cell, representing a highly organized structure. Each individual page, while containing an image, also expresses the sorted and ranked values through distribution of images in the browser window. In effect, while screenshooting, the artist records the changing data values that organize and render the image visible on the internet.

Internet images are infrastructural and indexical and as such they are geopolitical sites mapping politics, techniques, design, and neoliberal structures as forces that govern the movement of images within the browser window. *Unerasable Images* makes use of a white space, also known as negative space,[5] to trace one single image, the thumbnail image of the Lego Tank Man. With the negative space the artwork marks what normally is not a visible element of the internet, namely its infrastructures that contain geopolitics of data circulation, internet censorship, and computational processes. The materiality of image (re)production and its infrastructural distribution is mapped in the artwork by erasing all other images and clearly marking the Lego Tank Man's route across the picture frame. Paradoxically, by erasing all images but one, *Unerasable Images* poetically unfolds the forces that operate and reconfigure images as entangled with parameters of visibility, optimization algorithms, and operational interfaces. In effect *Unerasable Images* is a map that traces the movement of the censored image across the internet, and it is a documentation of an artist performing what in China would be a censored act of searching for a forbidden image.

Chinese Censorship

The case of Chinese internet censorship is almost as long as the history of the internet in China. Three years after introducing the "free" internet, in 1997 the Chinese government imposed a comprehensive regulation stating that "individuals are prohibited from using the Internet to harm national security" (2010). Well-known technologies such as blocking IP addresses and web domains have been used since then to limit or completely prohibit access to many Western domains and web portals such as Wikipedia, Google, Facebook, and many more. Apart from blocking platforms that are outside Chinese borders, the internet is controlled at a domestic level with the use of various content-filtering techniques. While censorship can be defined as an information control across and within borders, resulting in the denial of access to information (Dowell 2006; Li 2004), the consequences, conditions, and implications of censorship online are highly complex. Fan Yang describes censorship on the internet as "a mechanism of dis-appearance, which combines algorithm[s] and human censors to *make invisible* what cannot be [seen]" (2016, original emphasis). The use of the image of the Lego Tank Man in *Unerasable Images* makes visible what cannot be seen. While image is displayed as part of the artwork, we trace technological and geopolitical conditions of its (dis)appearances by focusing on two problems of visibility on the internet that we identify: the difference between legitimate and illegitimate circulation of the image on the internet, and the boundary of what is visible or not and how it can be seen.

Geopolitics of Accessing the Internet

The Lego Tank Man image, while relevant in our discussion because of its political symbolism, shows what is technically possible on the Chinese internet and what is likely legitimate (or not) content. The image is also helpful in tracing how access to the internet in China changed over time. It first appeared on a Chinese web portal called 网易 (163.com) owned by NetEase, founded in 1997, the year when the term "Great Firewall" was coined to define Chinese reconstitution of the internet into state-governed space (Barme and Ye 1997). NetEase is a Chinese Internet technology company providing e-commerce platforms, video games, and infotainment content. Historically, the domain 163.com refers to dial-up services provided by China Telecom of the early internet era, in which users dialed 1-6-3 to connect to the internet over a telephone line, prior to the proliferation of broadband infrastructure in China (Zhou 2006, 138–39). Dialling 1-6-3 to a modem and typing 163.com with a keyboard allowed one to connect to cyberspace and surf the web via a computer interface. The action of typing (as if dialing) marked the moment of crossing a legitimated boundary and entering into regulated Chinese cyberspace.

Passing from the slow dial-up internet to a faster broadband reconfigures what can be seen online and how. Heavier data, more content, and frequent updates ushered in dynamic web pages that replaced static HTML sites and with broadband connection, web portals were able to offer more dynamic and real-time multimedia content. Indeed, "any image on a screen is a programmable image" that affords a particular kind of navigation and way of viewing the world (Hoelzl and Marie 2015, 132). The speed and capacity of the internet services change the way people engage with cyberspace spatially and temporally with dynamic computational-generated sites, heavier files, and faster data retrieval and rendering capability. But under the regulation in China, all web portals are required to exercise information control, especially the identification and removal of inappropriate content, such as politically sensitive content. For example, several international news outlets have reported that the comment functions on the news platform on 163.com were suspended (He 2020; Harper 2020). NetEase was fined by the state because "the company repeatedly allowed reader comments on news articles that were in violation of laws and regulations or relevant rules" (He 2020). In order to avoid inappropriate content, the state punishes those who own the platform. This means that domestic companies are subject to legal and financial consequences. Platform owners (not only internet service providers) are required to comply more strictly with state regulations, which results in companies having to censor so-called inappropriate content on their platforms to avoid punishment and fines. China exercises strict national security laws to control circulation of information, and any materials (including text and images) that harm national interests, spread rumors, and disrupt the social order are prohibited. Most companies stay cautious even though there is no clear definition of what it exactly means to harm national interests (this is often termed as tne red line). This is also the reason why we use the term "legitimate boundary" throughout the article, alluding to the vagueness, uncertainties, and constantly shifting of (hidden) rules in which something can be made legitimate or prohibited within a very short timeframe.

While censorship is a leading form of content moderation on web portals in China, it is expected that all companies comply, whether they are local or international. Those not complying with state requirements are blocked easily. Google is a case in point. The company had launched a Chinese-language version of Google search in 2000 and the China's domain (Google.cn) in 2006. At that time, Google occupied around one third of the search engine market share in China (Sheehan 2018). However, four years after entering China, Google announced that they stopped censoring search results by redirecting all search queries from Google.cn (China domain) to Google.com.hk (Hong Kong domain). Once it was redirected to a domain outside of mainland China, it became, arguably, a legitimized solution to avoid exercising censorship (Jiang 2014, 2). Here boundaries are uncertain and potentially negotiable with just the change and redirection of the domain from .cn to .hk at the technical and visible levels. This is one example of internet geopolitics showing unclear legal relation between cyber-space, technical operation of redirection, and geographic territory. The intention was to shift the "censorship burden" to the Chinese territory and its government (Jiang 2014, 2). With its independent judicial power and basic law at the time, Hong Kong's internet regulations were different from China's, with more freedom of expression and with no internet censorship. Therefore, redirect-ing the internet domain implies a possible change of regulation and censorship practice. However, Google's efforts to continue business in China and to escape self-censorship by moving to the free territory with laws independent of China was unsuccessful, resulting in blocking all access to Google search sites and appli-cations. Today, Google.com and Google.com.hk can be accessed from many other geographical locations but not from mainland China. The examples of NetEase and Google, while showing what content is and is not legible in China, show geopolitics as an issue of internet sovereignty with state borders demarcating the change in the rule of information flow and with censorship as a technique and a framework for controlling the internet and the web.

Censoring the (Toy) Image

Some content does manage to get through and stays visible online for a limited period of time. The Lego Tank Man, published on the car channel of 163.com as part of the Children's Day campaign, is an example of an image smuggled into the public domain in China. On May 31, 2013, 163.com published more than 130 pictures in the form of an image gallery slideshow, with the aim to showcase different types of nostalgic car toys. Many visitors to the website saw the image of the Lego Tank Man and left messages explaining the history of June Fourth and often praising the NetEase's editor's fearless actions of posting (*New Tang Dynasty Television* 2013; *Epoch Times* 2013; Tang 2013). While the image only survived (visible to the public) for half of a day, a typical lifetime for an image before removal,[6] it was enough time to be seen by visitors to the portal and to be picked up by servers beyond China. Instead of using the technique of drawing black marks on the text and images,[7] NetEase had chosen to erase the online image entirely by seamlessly skipping that particular slide. Unlike having the censor bars with blackout, the skip left no traces and no indication of what had been censored. This skip is hidden and unnoticeable.

The image is being taken down from NetEase because of its political nature, an unwanted image within the Chinese internet sovereignty. Beyond information control that has been mentioned, another purpose of censorship in China "is to reduce the probability of collective action by clipping social ties whenever any collective movements are in evidence or expected" (King, Pan, and Roberts 2013, 1). In this way, one of the criteria to for categorizing an image as politically sensitive is its potential for inspiring collective action. This may mean generating collective and commemorative events/actions that lead to viral effects of posting and sharing on the internet. With different messages already left on the site that were very close to the anniversary of June Fourth, this might have generated a viral effect of posting historical events, gathering people, and discussing the sensitive topic, which is regarded as unwanted consequences. Internet images might be politically sensitive and unwanted, and they might generate unwanted consequences. The image of Lego Tank Man has an unsettling status, consisting of certain censoring forces, while some images have a higher potential to generate collective actions.

What is unusual in case of the image circulation is that it was published by the NetEase platform and not by an individual user, an incident also noticed by the foreign websites, portals, and press within the same week, such as Ntdtv, Epochtimes, Apple Daily Hong

Kong, and BuzzFeed News.(*New Tang Dyansty Television* 2013; *Epoch*
Times 2013; Apple Daily 2013; Tang 2013). Censorship in China has
been implemented "at all levels of government—central, provincial
and local," with up to one thousand censors privately employed for
each individual site (King, Pan, and Roberst 2013, 1), and so publishing any materials on the web by the portal's editor represents a
boundary of legitimation and a confirmation of content as safe and
valid for publication. Suffice to say, self-censorship by the editors
is needed to judge the boundary of the red line. On the one hand,
the fact that the Tank Man composition is made with colorful Lego
toy bricks might suggest the triviality of the image and its toy-like
quality as a legitimate reason for publishing. But publication of
this image, on the other hand, suggests a deliberate decision,
because the image composition of a Tank Man is too obvious and
yet remarkable. Margaret Hillenbrand describes the "doubleness"
of an image's nature (2017, 147). These kinds of sensitive images
are not only entertaining and humorous but also have the ability
to transmit taboo information, especially under such a restricted
culture like in China (147). Tellingly, the Lego Tank Man image was
first published on a toy car channel of a Chinese web portal. This
double nature of the image has added another complexity beyond
just a literally sensitive image. Would this double nature of the
image render a different kind of visibility on the (Chinese) Internet?

The internet affords accessible search and easier reappropriation, as images are much easier to find. Internet images can be
downloaded, reproduced, uploaded, and published on different
servers and web pages as poor images (Steyerl 2009), circulating
on the internet seamlessly and widely across geopolitical sites. As
Hito Steyerl notes, "poor images are poor because they are heavily
compressed and travel quickly" (2009). When compared with print
media, internet images are different in terms of their materiality
and specificities. For example, they are lower in resolution and
smaller in size under sharing culture, which Steyerl refers to as the
source of "poor materials" for further composition, remixing, and
reappropriation (2009). This poor image, a scene made with toy

bricks and a minifigure, stands in sharp contrast to the realness, seriousness, and heaviness of the original Tank Man photograph. The specific double nature of the reappropriated Tank Man photograph further points to the materiality of images that are published and circulated within, and beyond, the restricted internet. It is argued that the double and poor nature of the image allows a different kind of visibility—the toy image is made visible via the platform, and it was not immediately censored.

To understand the situation of how such an image comes into existence, and how one gets to see it, we highlight, in this section, the complexity of the Chinese censorship that impacts how things, like a site or an image, are made (in)visible. There are no clear rules on what exactly can be seen, in which the legitimate boundary is constantly being tested and shifted, as seen in the case of the .hk/.cn Google domains and the Lego Tank Man image. Specifically, there is a temporal and spatial tension between the need for censoring and control, as well as the nature and specificity of the internet image. First is the double nature of the Lego Tank Man image that allows certain ambiguity and visibility. Second is the notion of the poor image that facilitates a quicker and wider circulation. Within such a short visible timeframe, the image is being published, discussed, reported, captured, erased, skipped, and more importantly, leaked beyond the Chinese internet territory. The publication of the image by NetEase, regardless if it is done as an act of refusal to self-censor or not, plays with the dual nature of the image, thus revealing that what constitutes an image's legitimacy can be temporarily unclear.

Internet Images

Internet images carry the residue of their making, which is technological, material, social, conceptual, and aesthetic. The networked conditions of internet images are not visible on the screen and such images need to be analyzed also as material objects (Gaboury 2021). Strictly speaking, internet images are computer graphic images but not the kind most often associated with "spectacular visual effects and lifelike simulations in film, television, and digital games" (Gaboury 2021, 3). To reiterate, the internet images that we refer to are those that circulate over the networks as thumbnail images appearing in image search results, or those published on web pages, platforms, and similar networked locations. What we see in the moment of observing an internet image in a browser window is an act of image retrieval. This de facto highly localized and networked image construction always depends on network conditions that govern the quality of the retrieved image, the speed of retrieval, not to mention the variety of representations and forms, from memes to fakes, animated gifs, and many others. The version of the browser and graphics card in the computer also determine how the image is rendered. And, as the example of the Lego Tank Man in *Unerasable Images* shows, the location from which the image is sought and accessed also counts. The internet image is a composite of the image and its infrastructures in relations.

This rich environment in which internet images circulate keeps urgent the question of what images are, because the boundaries between different kinds of images are drawn and redrawn continuously. The family of images, a taxonomy of images proposed by W. J. T. Mitchell (1984), which organizes them into five categories, expands; and beyond graphic, optical, perceptual, mental, and verbal images, others appear, such as networked images (Dewdney and Sluis 2022) or computational images of various kinds. Indeed, more recently images have been defined by taking into account automatic processes of their creation, available in contemporary technologies of digital image processing. These technologies replace optics with algorithms, and in effect, images become operative (Farocki 2004; Hoel 2018); that is, they perform functions other than being visually accessible to the human eye. For Ingrid Hoelzl and Remi Marie (2015), this operative character of images makes them close to software, as images become "ubiquitous, infinitely adaptable and adaptive, and something intrinsically merged with software" (2015, 7). The malleability of images, defined by Hoelz and Marie as "illusion of an image," is the result of various techniques and technologies that are used in the production of images. The use of still images to make a film conveys "the illusion of movement" (2015, 57). In the digital context, it is replaced by another type of movement that turns images into "nothing but the moment of network access" (2015, 126). Movement still takes place, but in the form of transfer and communication bandwidth between data servers and computers. This is no longer an optical operation, but one where the operative character of softimages relates to their programmable function as objects in "relational space" of urban dataspace that can be computed, accessed, and that circulate. An image in this context becomes fluid, a relational object, a part of data transfer and network access that brings together physical space and data transmission, what we refer to as internet image.

Computers and related technologies radically changed how images are made, how they circulate, and how they are consumed, but also who and what is part of these processes beyond the human actors. Mitchell (1984) says that images

> are not just a particular kind of sign, but something like
> an actor on the historical stage, a presence or character
> endowed with legendary status, a history that parallels
> and participates in the stories we tell ourselves about
> our own evolution from creatures "made in the image"
> of a creator to creatures who make themselves and their
> world in their own image. (504)

The Lego Tank Man is such a presence that tells the story of the tragic past events, and it provokes speculations on how it was possible for this image to enter the highly censored territory of the Chinese internet. The image crosses political and geographic borders that configure the image as (in)visible through the complexity of governance, history, humans, and machines. *Unerasable Images* guides the process of interpreting and analyzing how the image is situated; that is, where the image is and how it is computationally generated and removed. Once located within these networked infrastructures that are material, social, political, and geographical, the boundary of the image becomes highly volatile, especially as it is conditioned by networked protocols and computational technologies, while confirmed as legitimate for a short time. Internet images are always part of such relations that render them (in)visible.

Rather than being primarily a likeness, a representation, or an optical counterpart of an object created by reflecting or refracting, Mitchell theorizes an image as a complex object that is present historically. But if images have power (Freedberg 1991), if they act (Bakewell 1998; Bredekamp 2017), and desire (Mitchell 2005), then it is not just historical conditions that frame images as actors. Images are both objects and processes (Boehm and Mitchell 2009, 108), and they mark humans as distinct from other species because of their ability to conceptualize and abstract. In its most broad definition, after quattrocento artist Leon Battista Alberti, we can talk about images "as soon as naturally occurring entities evince a minimum of human intervention and elaboration" (Bredekamp 2017). Such intervention when generating internet images is quite complex, because it involves humans, and, as we have already shown, machines, and computational, and networked procedures, as well as geopolitical conditions.

Infrastructures of Seeing

Unerasable Images captures an otherwise censored image, and frames infrastructures that make it visible, or not, in the browser. In this way the artwork creates conditions of seeing the internet images. On one hand it makes visible the censored image, and on the other it records the artist's network location that had enabled (or not) seeing the image. The screenshots captured result from relation between the artist and the image within the network at the moment of screenshooting. *Unerasable Images* documents the act of searching for the Lego Tank Man image, and records, collects, and archives screenshots into an animated video. Searching for the image in computational terms refers to the process of information retrieval. To query something from a massive database requires defining its parameters in order to retrieve data based on certain criteria. In this process, algorithms select, sort, and prioritize data from databases of more than 10 billion images. In other words, using image search engines activates an algorithmic process of arranging images in response to the various intentions and queries from users, with results displayed on a web page. Common reasons to use the Google Image Search engine include searching for specific images, for the meaning of a word, when shopping or looking for inspiration, or simply for fun and to kill time.[8] Even if reasons to use Google Image Search are trivial, it is a significant infrastructure that serves more than 3.5 billion searches per day, influencing what is or is not visible on the internet. *Unerasable Images* operates through the capture of these moments, where the image is made legitimate by tracing the route that the censored image takes across search-results page. Artistic intervention marks different moments in this automated process collecting and visualizing its results.

During the exhibition *Screenshots: Desire and Automated Image* (Tyżlik-Carver 2019), curated by one of the authors, the work was installed not as a video projection but as a mechanical recreation of automated processes of image retrieval. The gallery installation used the carousel slide projector with a selection of eighty slides displayed on the gallery wall one by one (see Figure 1.3) with each slide showing one screenshot of a browser window and the Lego Tank Man on it. The remaining screenshots were organized and stored in the wooden slide boxes attached to the wall next to the projected images. In this installation the projection retains its relatively small size, almost keeping to the usual dimensions of a computer monitor, which might suggest a secondary importance of the image to its apparatus. The image is definitely not unimportant, but this arrangement reveals a somewhat incidental nature of the image that is dependent on the workings of the machine. On

[Figure 1.3]. The installation view of *Unerasable Images* during the exhibition *Screenshots: Desire and Automated Image.* Copyright 2019 by Winnie Soon; courtesy of the artist.

one hand, what is displayed, in what order, and for how long had been already defined by the artist, and the machine executes this operation.

The diagram of algorithmic sorting of slides shows the design of the operation on display at the gallery (see Figure 1.4). This model reconfigures computations that generate internet images into an algorithm for sorting slides to be projected in the gallery. Slides are sorted into four batches each representing a different image class, and each is to follow a number of procedures until the process halts at the point of reaching the state "counter = 0." The installation makes apparent operations that make *Unerasable Images,* such as gathering, classifying, organizing, and displaying spatial data, and the diagram becomes a cartographic description of these procedures and illustrates granularity and materiality of internet images. The use of a carousel mimics mechanically a binary process of image production, including up-and-down slide changes and the off-and-on lamp switch. The sound effects of temporal switching, the pauses for slide changes that synchronize the appearances and disappearances of the visual projection on the wall add further depth to the diagram and its mechanics. All three relational elements, orderly slides, the mechanical device, and projected images, resonate with what we have demonstrated throughout this article, that internet images are spatial and technological constructions. To ask what the internet image is or where the boundary of images is, we suggest looking beyond representation and propose a cartographic reading that pays attention to the operation of spaces and the relationality between them. The viewer enters this space through the architectural organization of the *Unerasable Images.*

Internet images are far from being different in this respect. However, while in the creation of perspective an artist's control over the relation between the image and its viewer is clear, in the internet image, as we have shown, this relation is distributed across different actors such as the complex networked infrastructures of search engines and other algorithmic and data-based operations. However, *Unerasable Images* reclaims the artist's control to reveal infrastructural conditions that are inscribed in the circulation of internet images including the Lego Tank Man. The problem of perspective was the issue of representation of three-dimensional space on a two-dimensional surface. The issue that internet images address is how to make visible the entanglement of technological, political, geographic, and social conditions that actively participate in retrieving the internet images. The moment of making the internet image is the moment of its retrieval as it circulates across infrastructural conditions.

While images change and are redefined formally as a result of concepts such as softimage, networked image, operational image, and others, what can be said about the image depends on what it represents and how it is made. How to see the image then depends on techniques used for its making and how it appears in the world. While

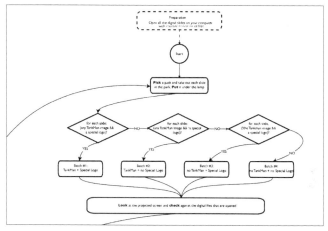

[Figure 1.4]. A portion of the algorithmic diagram of the sorting slides. Copyright 2019 by Winnie Soon; courtesy of the artist. The complete diagram is available at https://siusoon.net/doc/files/BoundaryImg_algorithmicDiagram.jpg.

perspective or optics make images more realistic, operative quality of images understood as functioning in the wider computational systems brings another dimension and, in effect, other nonhuman subjects as those who also make and "see" images. Internet images reveal to us their dependence on networked infrastructures and their computational or "soft" character. While softimages evidence the unstable character of contemporary images as data-to-data operations, internet images introduce geopolitical and infrastructural conditions in which such images operate. And, while distributed and circulating across socio-technological networks, internet images also trace the networked space that makes them accessible to human eyes or leaves them within the confines of the networks.

Cyberspace is a territory inhabited by data, machines, code, images, user operations, texts, artistic interventions, deep-learning processes, and much else. It is a space of activities that reflect how this domain involves more than humans and their desires.

54 Cyberspace is a constructed and materially founded set of infra-structural systems that hold and process an increasing amount of information while being sustained by human and automated labor and various human–computer interactions. *Unerasable Images* captures its ambiguity revealed by the operation of looking for the Lego Tank Man, thus tracing the movement of data across systems and bodies across borders, all enabled by technological operations. These are geopolitical operations that the artwork brings into a frame, amalgamating physical locations and geographical coordinates with their data to project an image that refuses to disappear even if it is not visible—an internet image. The situation of getting an internet image involves processes of rendering data into images in the browser and responding to queries via search engine, to mention only two. These computational processes destabilize borders that traditionally contain an image. Daily repetition of the same gesture, Ctrl+PrtSc/Command+shift+4, over the period of one year, creates continuity that also disturbs the discrete nature of computational operations and undoes the boundaries of cyber-space as computational only. But perhaps we always knew that cyberspace is a composite of relations that are not just computa-tional and data based.

What we have done throughout this chapter is a cartographic reading of *Unerasable Images,* tracing it as a boundary image that frames the terrain on which internet images appear and disappear. We make visible and define the internet image and the many rela-tions that condition its making. As the title of this chapter suggests, our starting point was to treat *Unerasable Images* as a territory that bears traces of the many connections—technological, social, politi-cal, historical—that have been made in the making of this artwork. And so we read this work as a map of sorts with which to relate to and hold on to various forms of knowledge that each of us brings to this reading. We use the term "legitimate boundary" throughout the article to show how the boundary is constantly shifting spatially and temporarily and to trace what boundaries are crossed as the image circulates on the internet. Boundaries are many and they are always negotiated, even if they have been in place for a very long time. If the frame defines the borders of the image, *Unerasable Images* is a practical example of how they are easily dissolved while also often hard to define.

Notes

1   The term *screenshooting* refers to an artistic method to produce screenshots that capture unstable and impermanent archives (Schorr and Soon 2020; Soon and Schorr 2022).

2   The official reported numbers from China were around three hundred protesters killed and seven thousand wounded. However, there are also leaked secret documents that suggest a much higher death toll of at least ten thousand people. See the National Security Archive at https://nsarchive2.gwu.edu/NSAEBB/NSAEBB16/index.html and the online "8964 Museum" here: https://8964museum.com/time/t-h01-2-003?cate=1989.06.06.

3   "Advanced: How Search Works." https://developers.google.com/search/docs/advanced/guidelines/how-search-works.

4   "Advanced: How Search Works."

5   Negative space is a compositional feature in images. For another discussion of negative space in the context of the internet and as a network feature, see Tyžlik-Carver 2021.

6   According to King, Pan, and Roberts (2013, 5), major censorship activity happens within twenty-four hours on the social media platform Weibo regarding the topics related to Shanghai Subway Crash, Bo Xilai, and Gu Kailai. The twenty-four-hour period for censorship is confirmedl by analyzing the censored data from Weiboscope, a data-collection and visualization project developed by Dr. Fu King Wa from the University of Hong Kong. See https://weiboscope.jmsc.hku.hk/latest.php.

7   Blackout is a common cultural and artistic technique to address censorship. In 2010, hundreds of Australian websites faded their websites to black to protest against the government's web censorship agenda (Moses 2010). Within the particular context of Chinese censorship, artists have worked with the techniques of blackout to address the issue of human rights and freedom of speech, see for example Kim Asendorf's *Censored Censorship* (Hancock 2011) and Winnie Soon's *Unerasable Characters III* (Soon 2021).

8   See Peter Linsley 2009. Google Image Search: https://www.youtube.com/watch?v=h2Zaj0CAUoU.

References

Allen, Matthew. 2016. "Representing Computer-Aided Design: Screenshots and the Interactive Computer circa 1960." *Perspectives on Science* 24, no. 6: 637–68.

Andaluz, César, Escudero. 2012. *File_Món.* Accessed March 10, 2022. https://escudero andaluz.com/2012/08/07/file_mon/.

Ash, James, Rob Kitchin, and Agnieszka Leszczynski. 2018. "Digital Turn, Digital Geographies?" *Progress in Human Geography* 42, no. 1: 25–43.

Apple Daily. 2013. "内地網破禁「勇擋坦克」圖片驚現 借兒童節悼六四." *Apple Daily*, June 3. Accessed March 10, 2022. https://ipfs.io/ipfs/Qmdig4NtBTbUiw9KRri83 Warmrp4f5PFFFZMoQUwqXuNbZ/20130603/WIHZCTPWAG43OSDGBQZ7PKAGYE/ index.html.

Bakewell, Liza. 1998. "Image Acts." *American Anthropologist* 100, no. 1: 22–32.

Barad, Karen. 2007. *Meeting the Universe Halfway: Quantum Physics and the Entanglement of Matter and Meaning.* Durham. N.C.: Duke University Press Books.

Barme, Geremie R., and Sang Ye. 1997. "The Great Firewall of Chir.a." *Wired,* June 1. Accessed March 10, 2022. https://www.wired.com/1997/06/china-3/.

Bifet, Albert, Carlos Castillo, Paul-Alexandru Chirita, and Ingmar Weber. 2005. "An Analysis of Factors Used in Search Engine Ranking." In *Workshop on Adversarial Information Retrieval on the Web* (synopsis), 48–57. https://www.cs.upc.edu/~abifet/ analysis_SE_ranking.pdf.

Boehm, Gottfried, and W. J. T. Mitchell. 2009. "Pictorial versus Iconic Turn: Two Letters." *Culture, Theory and Critique* 50, no. 2–3: 103–21.

Bredekamp, Horst. 2017. *Image Acts: A Systematic Approach to Visual Agency.* Berlin: De Gruyter.

Burns, Ryan. 2021. "Transgressions: Reflecting on Critical GIS and Digital Geographies." *Digital Geography and Society* 2 (March). https://doi.org/10.1016/j.diggeo .2021.100011.

Brin, Sergey, and Lawrence Page. 1998. "The Anatomy of a Large-Scale Hypertextual Web Search Engine." *Computer Networks and ISDN Systems* 30, no. 1–7: 107–17.

Casey, Edward S. 2004. "Public Memory in Place and Time." In *Framing Public Memory,* ed. Kendall R. Philips, 17–44. Tuscaloosa: University of Alabama Press.

Chun, Wendy Hui Kyong. 2008. *Control and Freedom: Power and Paranoia in the Age of Fiber Optics.* Cambridge, Mass.: MIT Press.

Coconuts Hong Kong. 2018. "People around the World Pose as 'Tank Man' to remember June 4." COCONUTS, June 4. Accessed March 10, 2022. https://coconuts.co/ hongkong/news/people-around-the-world-pose-as-tank-man-to-remember -june-4/.

Crawford, Kate, and Trevor Paglen. 2019. "Excavating AI: The Politics of Training Sets for Machine Learning." *Excavating AI.* www.excavating.ai.

Deibert, Ron. 2015. "The Geopolitics of Cyberspace after Snowden." *Current History* 114, no. 768: 9.

Deibert, Ronald J. 2008. "Black Code Redux: Censorship, Surveillance, and the Militarization of Cyberspace." *Digital Media and Democracy: Tactics in Hard Times,* ed. Megan Boler, 137–64. Boston: MIT Press.

Dewdney, Andrew, and Katrina Sluis, eds. 2022. *The Networked Image in Post-Digital Culture.* New York: Routledge.

Dowell, William Thatcher. 2006. "The Internet, Censorship, and China." *Georgetown Journal of International Affairs* 7:111.

Edwards, Paul, Geoffrey Bowker, Steven Jackson, and Robin Williams. 2009. "Introduction: An Agenda for Infrastructure Studies." *Journal of the Association for Information Systems* 10, no. 5: 364–74.

Epoch Times. 2013. "网易含蓄悼六四：人，不能永远消失." *epochtimes,* June 6. Accessed
March 10, 2022. https://www.epochtimes.com/gb/13/6/6/n3887868.htm.

Farocki, Harun. 2004. "Phantom Images." Translated by Brian Pool. *Public* 29:12–22.

Finn, Ed. 2017. *What Algorithms Want: Imagination in the Age of Computing.* Cambridge,
Mass.: MIT Press.

Franklin, Stuart. 2016. "How Stuart Franklin Took His Tank Man Photograph." *Phaid-
on.* Accessed March 10. 2022. https://www.phaidon.com/agenda/photography/
articles/2016/april/05/how-stuart-franklin-took-his-tank-man-photograph/.

Freedberg, David. 1991. *The Power of Images: Studies in the History and Theory of
Response.* Chicago: University of Chicago Press.

Fuller, Matthew. 2008. "Introduction. The Stuff of Software." In *Software Studies: A
Lexicon,* 1–13. Cambridge, Mass.: MIT Press.

Gaboury, Jacob. 2021. *Image Objects: An Archaeology of Computer Graphics.* Cambridge,
Mass.: MIT Press.

Galloway, Alexander R. 2004. *Protocol: How Control Exists after Decentralization.* Cambridge, Mass.: MIT Press.

Gibson, William. 1984. *Neuromancer.* New York: Ace Books.

Gibson, William. 1987. *Burning Chrome.* New York: Ace Books.

Google. n.d. "Advanced: How Search Works." Google Search Central. Accessed
March 10, 2022. https://developers.google.com/search/docs/advanced/guidelines/
how-search-works.

Goriunova, Olga. 2019. "The Digital Subject: People as Data as Persons." *Theory,
Culture & Society* 36, no. 6: 125–45.

Hancock, Mark. 2011. "Kim Asendorf. Censored Censored Chinese News."
Digimag 61, February 2. Accessed March 10, 2022. http://digicult.it/hacktivism/
kim-asendorf-censored-censored-chinese-news/.

Harper, Cindy. 2020. "China Fines Tech Company NetEase for Not Censoring Comments Enough." *Reclaim The Net,* October 13. Accessed March 10, 2022. https://
reclaimthenet.org/china-fines-tech-company-netease/.

He, HuiFeng. 2020. "Censorship in China: NetEase Fined for Carrying 'Inappropriate'
Comments on News Platforms." *The Star,* October 12. Accessed March 10, 2022.
https://www.thestar.com.my/tech/tech-news/2020/10/12/censorship-in-china
-netease-fined-for-carrying-inappropriate-comments-on-news-platforms.

Hillenbrand, Margaret. 2017. "Remaking Tank Man, in China." *Journal of Visual Culture*
16, no. 2: 127–66.

Hills, Carol. 2014. "25 years later, Tank Man Lives on as a Symbol of Courage—Just
Not in China." *The World,* June 5. Accessed March 10, 2022. https://theworld.org/
stories/2014-06-05/25-years-later-tank-man-lives-outside-china-potent-symbol
-courage-and-bravery.

Hoel, Aud Sissel. 2018. "Operative Images: Inroads to a New Paradigm of Media
Theory." In *Image, Action, Space,* edited by Luisa Feiersinger, Kathrin Friedrich,
andMoritz Queisner, 11–28. Berlin: De Gruyter.

58   Hoelzl, Ingrid, and Rémi Marie. 2015. *Softimage: Towards a New Theory of the Digital Image.* Chicago: Intellect Books.

Ibrahim, Yasmin. 2016. "Tank Man, Media Memory and Yellow Duck Patrol: Remembering Tiananmen on Social Media." *Digital Journalism* 4, no. 5: 582–96.

Jiang, Min. 2014. "The Business and Politics of Search Engines: A Comparative Study of Baidu and Google's Search Results of Internet Events in China." *New Media & Society* 16, no. 2: 212–33.

Jing, Yushi, and Shumeet Baluja. 2008. "Visualrank: Applying Pagerank to Large-Scale Image Search." *IEEE Transactions on Pattern Analysis and Machine Intelligence* 30, no. 11: 1877–90.

King, Gary, Jennifer Pan, and Margaret E. Roberts. 2013. "How Censorship in China Allows Government Criticism but Silences Collective Expression." *American Political Science Review* 107, no. 2: 326–43.

Kitchin, Rob, and Martin Dodge. 2011. *Code/Space: Software and Everyday Life.* Software Studies. Cambridge, Mass.: MIT Press.

Kittler, Friedrich A. 1992. *Discourse Networks 1800/1900.* Stanford, Calif.: Stanford University Press.

Kittler, Friedrich A. 1999. *Gramophone, Film, Typewriter.* Stanford, Calif.: Stanford University Press.

Lamont, Michèle, and Virág Molnár. 2002. "The Study of Boundaries in the Social Sciences." *Annual Review of Sociology* 28, no. 1: 167–95.

Larkin, Brian. 2018. "Promising Forms: The Political Aesthetics of Infrastructure." *The Promise of Infrastructure,* ed. Anand Nikhil, Gupta Akhil, and Appel Hannah, 175–202. Durham, N.C.: Duke University Press.

Lepawsky, Josh. 2015. "The Changing Geography of Global Trade in Electronic Discards: Time to Rethink the e-Waste Problem." *The Geographical Journal* 181, no. 2: 147–59.

Li, Charles. 2004. "Internet Content Control in China." *International Journal of Communications Law and Policy* 8, no. 1: 1–38.

Li, Zhilin. 1995. "An Examination of Algorithms for the Detection of Critical Points on Digital Cartographic Lines." *The Cartographic Journal* 32, no. 2: 121–25.

Lillemose, Jacob, and Mathias Kryger. 2015. "The (Re)Invention of Cyberspace." *Kunstkritikk* (blog). August 24, 2015. https://kunstkritikk.com/the-reinvention-of-cyber space.

Linsley, Peter. 2009. "Google Image Search." YouTube, March 2. Accessed March 10, 2022. https://www.youtube.com/watch?v=h2Zaj0CAUoU.

Mitchell, W. J. T. 1984. "What Is an Image?" *New Literary History* 15, no. 3: 503–37.

Mitchell, W. J. T. 2005. *What Do Pictures Want? The Lives and Loves of Images.* Chicago: University of Chicago Press.

Moses, Asher. 2010. "Websites Fade to Black in Censorship Protest." *The Sydney Morning Herald,* January 26. Accessed March 10, 2022. https://www.smh.com.au/technology/websites-fade-to-black-in-censorship-protest-20100126-mvsw.html.

New Tang Dyansty Television. 2013. "网易破禁 借六一纪念六四？" YouTube, June 4. Accessed March 10, 2022. https://www.youtube.com/watch?v=aBTcwAtc4fw.

Noble, Safiya Umoja. 2018. *Algorithms of Oppression.* New York: New York University Press.

Page, Lawrence, Sergey Brin, Rajeev Motwani, and Terry Winograd. 1999. *The Pagerank Citation Ranking: Bringing Order to the Web. Technical Report.* Stanford InfoLab. Accessed March 10, 2022. http://ilpubs.stanford.edu:8090/422/.

People's Daily Online. 2020. "The Internet in China." *People's Daily Online* [White paper], June 8. Accessed March 10, 2022. http://en.people.cn/90001/90776/90785/7017177.html.

Qiu, Jack Linchuan. 1999. "Virtual Censorship in China: Keeping the Gate between the Cyberspaces." *International Journal of Communications Law and Policy* 4, no. 1: 25.

Rabbani, Majid, and Paul W. Jones. 1991. *Digital Image Compression Techniques.* Bellingham, Wash.: SPIE Press.

Richelson, Jeffrey T. and Michael L. Evans. 1999. "Tiananmen Square, 1989: The Declassified History." *The National Security Archive,* June 1. Accessed March 10, 2022. https://nsarchive2.gwu.edu/NSAEBB/NSAEBB16/index.html

Ridgway, Renée. 2017. "Against a Personalisation of the Self." *Ephemera: Theory & Politics in Organization* 17, no. 2: 377–97.

Ridgway, Renée. 2021. Re:search: *The Personalised Subject vs. the Anonymous User.* Copenhagen Business School. PhD Series No. 21. Accessed March 10. 2022. https://research.cbs.dk/en/publications/research-the-personalised-subject-vs-the-anonymous-user.

Schorr, Sarah, and Winnie Soon. 2020. "Screenshooting Life Online: Two Artworks." In *Metaphors of the Internet: Ways of Being in the Age of Ubiquity,* ed. Annette N. Markam, and Katrin Tiidenberg, 175–181. New York: Peter Lang.

Shannon, Claud, and Warren Weaver. 1998. *The Mathematical Theory of Communication.* Urbana: University of Illinois Press.

Sheehan, Matt. 2018. "How Google Took on China—and Lost." *MIT Technology Review.* Accessed March 10, 2022. https://www.technologyreview.com/2018/12/19/138307/how-google-took-on-china-and-lost/.

Shehata, Omar. 2019. "Unraveling the JPEG." Edited by Matthew Colen, Fred Hohman, and Sara Stalla. ParametricPress, no. 1, *Science + Society* (April). https://doi.org/10.5281/zenodo.2655041.

64memo. 1989. "官方首次公布死傷人數." 8964museum.com, June 6. Accessed March 10, 2022. https://8964museum.com/time/t-h01-2-003/?cate=1989.06.06.

Snodgrass, Eric, and Winnie Soon. 2019. "API Practices and Paradigms: Exploring the Protocological Parameters of APIs as Key Facilitators of Sociotechnical Rorms of Exchange." *First Monday* 24, no. 2. https://doi.org/10.5210/fm.v24i2.9553.

Soon, Winnie. 2017. *Unerasable Images.* Artwork. http://siusoon.net/unerasable-images/.

Soon, Winnie. 2021. "The Unerasable Characters III." *The New River: A Journal of Digital Art and Literature* (Spring). Accessed March 10, 2022. https://thenewriver.us/775-2/.

Soon, Winnie, and Geoff Cox. 2020. *Aesthetic Programming: A Handbook of Software Studies.* London: Open Humanities Press.

Soon, Winnie, and Sarah Schorr. 2022. "Screenshooting Impermanence." In *Imperm-*

anence: *Exploring Continuous Change across Cultures,* ed. Haidy Geismar, Ton Otto, and Cameron David Warner, 292–304. London: UCL Press.

Steyerl, Hito. 2009. "In Defense of the Poor Image." *e-flux journal* 10, no. 11. https://www.e-flux.com/journal/10/61362/in-defense-of-the-poor-image/.

Sui, Daniel Z. 2004. "GIS, Cartography, and the 'Third Culture': Geographic Imaginations in the Computer Age." *The Professional Geographer* 56, no. 1: 62–72.

Tang, Kevin. 2013. "Chinese Netizens Defiantly Remember Tiananmen Square." *BuzzFeed,* June 3. Accessed March 10, 2022. https://www.buzzfeednews.com/article/kevintang/how-the-chinese-internet-remembers-tiananmen-on-its-24th-ann.

Thornton, Pip. 2017. "Geographies of (Con) Text: Language and Structure in a Digital Age." *Computational Culture* 6. http://computationalculture.net/geographies-of-context-language-and-structure-in-a-digital-age/.

Thornton, Pip. 2018. "A Critique of Linguistic Capitalism: Provocation/Intervention." *GeoHumanities* 4, no. 2: 417–37.

Thylstrup, Nanna Bonde, and Stina Teilmann. 2017. "Thumbnail Images: Uncertainties, Infrastructures, and Search Engines." *Digital Creativity* 28, no. 4: 279–96.

Tyżlik-Carver, Magdalena. 2019. *Screenshots: Desire and Automated Image.* Exhibition. Aarhus: Gelleri Image. https://www.galleriimage.dk/index.php/en/2019-udst-eng/1144-screenshots-desire-and-automated-image.

Tyżlik-Carver, Magdalena. 2021. "In Search of Common Forms and Curatorial Epistemologies. On the Exhibition OPEN SCORES: How to Program the Commons." *Aesthetics of the Commons,* edited by Cornelia Sollfrank, Felix Stalder, and Shusha Niederberger, 125–52. Zurich: diaphanes.

Tyżlik-Carver, Magdalena. 2022. "Screenshot Situations: Imaginary Realities of Networked Images." *The Networked Image in Post-Digital Culture,* edited by Andrew Dewdney and Katrina Sluis. New York: Routledge.

von Neuman, John. 1945. First Draft of a Report on the EDVAC. Available at https://web.mit.edu/STS.035/www/PDFs/edvac.pdf.

Han. 2011. "Contextual Weighting for Vocabulary Tree Based Image Retrieval." In *2011 International Conference on Computer Vision,* 209–16. IEEE. https://ieeexplore.ieee.org/document/6126244.

Wang, Yuan Cai. 2014. "人民日报权威论坛：网络主权，一个不容回避的议题." people.cn, June 23. Accessed March 10, 2022. http://opinion.people.com.cn/n/2014/0623/c1003-25183666.html.

Yang, Fan. 2016. "Rethinking China's Internet Censorship: The Practice of Recoding and the Politics of Visibility." *New Media & Society* 18, no. 7: 1364–81.

Zeng, Jinghan, Tim Stevens, and Yaru Chen. 2017. "China's Solution to Global Cyber Governance: Unpacking the Domestic Discourse of 'Internet Sovereignty.'" *Politics & Policy* 45, no. 3: 432–64.

Zhou, Yongming. 2006. *Historicizing Online Politics: Telegraphy, the Internet, and Political Participation in China.* Stanford, Calif.: Stanford University Press.

Zuboff, Shoshana. 2015. "Big Other: Surveillance Capitalism and the Prospects of an Information Civilization." *Journal of Information Technology* 30, no. 1: 75–89.

2

Real-Making with Boundary Images: Ethnographic Explorations of Far-Right Worlds

Melody Devries

So far, this book has explored various forms of boundary images and questioned how to study images beyond just their representations or their affects. In this chapter, I further this challenge by augmenting Star's (1989) "boundary object" to develop a new conceptual tool, the ontological boundary image. The ontological boundary image contributes to our broader understandings of how folks come to believe in what we might otherwise consider entirely illogical or imaginary beliefs about the world, such as that the election was stolen by a mysterious group of powerful elites or that Donald Trump is entangled in literal spiritual warfare. Many of these conspiracies emerge from white supremacist and anti-Semitic histories and social systems; their core narratives have been known for decades as untrue tools that foster hate. Yet while such beliefs are easy to write off within the liberal scientific world, these conspiracies are experienced as deeply true to adherents. They motivate grand actions and sacrifices, and they are nearly impenetrable by fact-checking techniques (Devries and Brett 2021).

It is precisely for these reasons that I argue that research about conspiracy should incorporate theorizations of spiritual belief. Conspiracies are not simply ideological principles or abstractions. Rather, like religious beliefs, conspiracies come to be felt within the bodies of adherents as undeniable realities about the form and function of the physical world (Luhrmann 2020).

As we establish in this book's Introduction, boundary images are lively entities composed of symbol, affect, data, and materials that provide infrastructures for translation processes. Boundary images enable relatability and movement between otherwise contradictory or conflicting interests or ideas. An *ontological* boundary image is thus a boundary image that enables travel between differing ontologies. This chapter presents an [auto]ethnographic analysis of my interactions with far-right and otherworldly images with the aim of highlighting the moments when I, as secular and antiracist ethnographer, feel my own ontology threatened against my will by prolonged interaction with conspiratorial images. As Bubandt (2014), Harding (1987), and others have described, interactions with potential manifestations of the otherworldly are sometimes enough to induce tinges of doubt in the stability of our world. It is within these fleeting interactions that the veil between worlds— the spiritual, the conspiratorial, and the physical or the "rational"— is thinned. By narrowing in on these moments, I avoid analyzing the content of images and instead focus on the dynamic moments during which an image and its various parts can accelerate the processes that convince or compel conspiratorial belief.

In what follows, I first theorize the processes that form belief and reify alternative worlds. As part of this, I include an historical overview of the ontological overlaps between the contemporary conspiratorial far-right and evangelical Christianity to emphasize that understanding one can become synonymous with under- standing the other. As the rise of Christian Nationalism in American culture and governance overtakes the short-lived rise of the so-called Alt-Right, the importance of understanding the shared processes of belief between far-right adherents and evangelicals cannot be underplayed. In the second part of this chapter ("Making Contact"), I develop the concept of the ontological boundary image in line with my theorization of belief-as-process. To demonstrate "ontological boundary images," I discuss my encounters with various images during ethnographic fieldwork that spanned the offline and the online (via physical pamphlets and literature, TikTok, Facebook, Parler, and Rumble). Engaging my positionality as an ethnographer suspended between academic, spiritual, and conspiratorial worlds helps show how spiritual-political convictions are continuously maintained through a series of interactions that formulate belief. Caught in "moments of real-making" (Luhrmann 2020), I show how images like the ones featured here become ontological boundary images, and help make the worlds depicted by far-right conspiracies tangibly real in an embodied way that renders such worlds undeniable to adherents, even in the face of evidence to the contrary or a prolonged unfulfillment of their predictions. Throughout, I forward that it is through matter—that is, material interactions made possible by a historic network of spiritual-political power—that harmful far-right and conspiratorial beliefs come to matter so much to adherents. Lastly, I want to recognize that my ethnographic experiences necessarily emerge in relation to my upbringing within white, Christian, supremacist worlds, all of which I will be working to deconstruct in my own life indefinitely. My goal with this chapter is to make practical use of my past and positionality in order to shed light on those processes that convict actual far right adherents today, so that we might better disrupt those processes in the future.

Belief as Process: Moments of Real-Making

To convey the function of the ontological boundary image, I first ask the reader to understand belief as a process as opposed to a static propositional commitment or set of abstract thoughts (Luhrmann 2020). I propose that ontological boundary images emerge and are at work during such a process.

In early 2020, the Twitter hashtag #raptureanxiety revealed that thousands of users shared (or used to share) a visceral fear of the pending rapture. The rapture refers to the moment when the saved (those who had accepted Jesus as their savior) would be caught up in rapid ascension to heaven, rising through the air and leaving the earth behind. While the rapture was supposed to be a joyous occasion, for many evangelical children raised in the 1980s and 1990s, it threatened the possibility of being "left behind" to endure God's tribulation. As one Twitter user expressed it: "I spent my childhood terrified of being left behind. I am told I accepted Jesus in my heart at 4; it didn't matter though. I would still pray the sinner's prayer often just in case the rapture happened. I never felt safe."

Admittedly, I have my own experience with rapture anxiety. Every so often when I was growing up, awaking from a nap or after playing alone in the basement for too long, I would find my parents missing. Frantically, I would search every room, the backyard, the garage. My heart pounded until I found them or until their car pulled back into the driveway. In the premillennialism I was raised with, those left behind would endure seven years of tribulation at the hands of variously horrifying beings: large flying locusts that sting like scorpions, demon creatures released from hell, and of course, Satan, The Beast, and the Antichrist. When people experience moments of rapture anxiety or panic, their body processes and responds to the vividly real feeling that God has left them behind, and that they will soon have to face the monsters of the apocalypse alone (see also Hartzler 2014).

Rapture anxiety highlights a critically important feature of belief: the extent that such beliefs about invisible beings and not-yet-present threats are felt from within the body. On top of this, rapture anxiety highlights how these fearful encounters with the not (yet) present mobilize actions that reaffirm the realness of the belief. When my own moments of rapture anxiety ended, my belief was not shaken but instead reinforced. Having been spared

this time, I would be compelled to read my Bible and seek more
reassurance that I would be ready "next time." I prayed the sinner's
prayer again and again, to avoid another "close call." In the process,
I developed a muscle memory of a certain future.

Belief in the unseen and the not (yet) present is often reimagined,
rehearsed, and purposefully made material in a variety of ways as a
means of cultivating the felt realness of that belief. In their analysis
of *the materiality of the rapture,* Kelly Baker (2011) writes about stu-
dents that were trained to get "rapture ready" through rehearsed
bodily actions during a summer Bible camp, such as being taught
to jump into the air. According to Baker's interlocutors, this activity
called *rapture practice* made it easier for the rapture to occur.
Perhaps, as all these children were caught in the air for a split
second, God might find it a bit easier to initiate the rapture. In a
more extreme version, GodTube videos document young men and
women caught within a system of bungee cords and pulleys. Here,
young people are shot into the air in sharp and jarring movement
(Baker 2011). Rather than induce the rapture, this scene was meant
to give participants a tangible feeling of a belief that had not yet
arrived. Understandably, this method cultivated a very palpable
terror and exhilaration within participants (Baker 2011, 103).

The eschatology of evangelical Christianity follows a biblical literalism that describes events that occur in the physical world as either
driven by spiritual events and beings, and/or as evidence of the
impending end times. The rapture and all its characters, however,
remain invisible; they cannot be confirmed as real in the same way
something like our family or church can. In such conditions, rapture
practices are meant to both mimic and to reify the imminence of
invisible beings and events that are otherwise difficult to conceive
of as real in the way required by Biblical literalist preachers and
prophets. In other words, rapture practice gives materiality and
therefore realness to an otherwise invisible, intangible belief.
As Baker (2011, 103) writes: "bodies in the air make ascension
tangible."

Of course, jumping or being launched into the air does not alone keep one's belief in the rapture vivid. Apart from embodied rehearsals of belief, interaction with media objects like books, websites, and other digital and print documentations and timelines of the impending apocalypse also help make the imminence of the rapture vivid and material (Baker 2011). Folks may encounter the rapture through YouTube or TikTok videos, or through best-selling books like Pastor John Hagee's *Four Blood Moons* (2013) or the *Left Behind* (1995–2007) fiction series by pastors and Tim LaHaye and Jerry B. Jenkins. For adherents, these interactions with technologies like books, websites, or videos cultivated the (often short-lived) feeling of being rapture ready within a physical world that could end at any moment, while at the same time cultivating the felt need to continuously renew such readiness (Baker 2011).

This emphasis on the recurrent, interactive materiality of belief resonates with Tanya Luhrmann's (2020) model of belief as an embodied process. To Luhrmann (2020), mundane actions or ritu-alized practices of "real-making" like reading the Bible or attending prayer groups make up the lived experience of belief, facilitating a process of becoming into a specific spiritual reality during everyday life. Belief is thus never quite complete, but rather an ongoing set of practices that adherents must keep up. Confident belief or con-viction in the unseen and extraordinary is thus maintained by *work* that requires interactions with a variety of objects and entities. It is not something that is ever achieved or finished in a single moment, or something that we should conceptualize as static or unwavering, despite its appearance as such. In this approach, we can think of acts of devotion not as reactions to already-entirely formed belief but as part of the process that continuously makes belief felt-as-real in an experiential and embodied way (Luhrmann 2020). Critically, this approach to belief highlights two things: (1) That processes that form belief are in themselves an element of spiritual and/or ideological recruitment that can be studied, and (2) that belief must be understood as a lived reality brought to life daily, as opposed to a static, one-time propositional commitment.

This approach to belief is deeply applicable to the study of contemporary far-right political belief, its tendency toward conspiracy, and its capacity to mobilize adherents to pursue actions against invisible threats. While evangelicals encountered the rapture through books, sermons, websites, and make-shift trebuchets, far-right adherents similarly encounter the conspiratorial through various online websites, television, and other media content. I argue that these interactions and practices don't just signify abstract belief but help to materialize an experiential reality different from ours, or an alternative world. To adherents, these alternative worlds have different metaphysical systems and are often characterized by their inclusion of invisible beings and imminent threats.

In this alternative world, far-right or conspiratorial adherents exist tangibly alongside invisible beings and extraordinary circumstances (such as the end times, or QAnon's "Storm"), which they experience as physically ongoing and/or propagating imminent danger. Importantly, I use "world" here not in the culturally relative or subjective sense, where we would consider people within a certain cultural or subcultural group as incorrectly projecting an interpretation onto an objectively existing "actual" world, the one we all occupy (Bubandt 2014). Rather, and in alignment both with the ontological turn in anthropology (e.g., Viverios de Castro 2004) and Nelson Goodman's 1978 philosophical interpretation of irrealism, I treat these alternative experiential realities as world-versions that come to life when they are called into existence repeatedly and consistently through material relations (actions or interactions) between people, objects, concepts, or images and representations. The imminence of the rapture becomes and simultaneously maintains its felt realness in moments where its features (e.g., parental absence, physical ascendance into the sky) are materialized, and thus allow the belief to be embodied and interacted with, however briefly. It is here that adherents feel and experience an alternative reality. The recurrence of such instances allows adherents to maintain their occupation of a time and space that is different from ours as nonbelievers or academic researchers. Here, supernatural or otherwise invisible forces operate amid the tangible.

Evidence that adherents of the far-right conspiracy QAnon experience extraordinary, invisible, and/or supernatural beings as active within the world they inhabit was demonstrated in November 2021, when more than one hundred people gathered in Texas where President John F. Kennedy was assassinated in hopes that his deceased son JFK, Jr. (and a variety of other celebrities) would reappear and declare Trump as the rightful U.S. president (Williams & Marfin 2021). Importantly, an irrealist model considers such actions not simply as "crazy" or misguided interpretations of how the world works but rather allows us to theorize how such adherents come to occupy a time and space that feels just as real and authentic as our own skeptical world. To work within an irrealist framework thus means to not pathologize the far-right adherent as simply naïve, foolish, or always already extreme, since to do so inevitably neglects the fact that socializations within mainstream systems of white supremacy resemble and/or are linked to the production of such alternative worlds. In bypassing assertion of the "realness" or lack thereof in such claims during our study, an irrealist approach allows us to "take seriously" the fact that the felt reality of conspiratorial adherents is shaped by social processes not unlike the ones that allow us to trust our own epistemologies and conceptions about the world. As well, it allows us to adjust our analytical lens toward those processes of conspiratorial worldmaking as they emerge from everyday life within supremacist social systems.

Taking Seriously

Importantly, to talk of "alternative worlds" and irrealism is not to say that we can make no claims about the actual world or that no reality or truth exists. Empirical knowledge and truths exist about the roundness of the Earth, for example. Similarly, research from the social sciences and the work of activists prove that historical inequalities and institutionalized prejudices continue to produce immense, tangible, very real oppressions for people of color, Queer people, women, and working-class people. It is this empirical truth that motivates our study into the harmful formations of the far-right.

This considered, I propose we might learn new things about what compels belief in conspiracy and harmful politics by using an irrealist model to "take far-right adherents seriously." By this, I do not mean that we should seriously consider or debate the ideas proposed by the far-right and/or conspiracy theorists. Nor do I imply that scholars, journalists, and activists alike do not already take the threat that contemporary fascism and disinformation pose to marginalized people and democratic systems seriously. Instead, "taking seriously" in this context means treating belief in the unseen, unknowable, or otherwise unbelievable things not as incorrect or foolish empirical knowledge for the time being but instead as maintained ontological knowledge: something that comes to be known through one's embodied way of being in the world. In the same way one knows a friend or family member's love is real in their everyday life, an adherent of the far-right conspiracy QAnon *knows* that God and the demonic exist, or that Trump will be reinstated as president by divine intervention. These everyday "truths" shape how folks operate and make choices in the world. It affects the Facebook pages they seek out or the subscriptions they sign up for.

This framework allows us to consider how adherents might experience various levels of conviction at various moments. For example, one's belief in God may become stronger during a worship service but fade in intensity during the week. Similarly, one's belief in a conspiracy may be lessened when one neglects going online and engages with their "nonbeliever" family more often. In this sense, taking seriously also means not assuming that a spiritual or conspiratorial world is something experienced homogeneously by a specified group and that can therefore be explained as the symptom of some underlying problem or social condition that uniformly affects the whole group. In other words, this approach allows us to take account of the complexities and variations that exist underneath the stereotype of the "brainwashed conspiracy theorist." As pointed out by Venturini (2021), contemporary far-right and conspiratorial culture in the United States and Canada has been treated by recent scholarship as adjacent or descendant from online meme and trolling culture (e.g., from Phillips 2015 to Beren 2019 and Wendling 2018). Conspiracy theories and the memeing of the broadly identifiable online alt-right is thus easily, like older iterations of conspiracy, "dismissed, denounced, and canonized" (Hebdige 1979, pg 2) as mischievous threats to normative society and mature democratic process (Venturini 2021). In terms of the contemporary conspiratorial and Christian nationalist far-right, this lack of taking seriously is no doubt exacerbated by the often outrageous or convoluted appearance of conspiratorial, far-right, and otherwise "prophetic" media content, which we on the outside might perceive as carrying flimsy, amateur, or absurd arguments and contradictory reasoning. However, an alternative approach is to understand these conspiracies as describing *entirely coherent alternative ontologies* (ways of being in the world) that are constructed and maintained through material interactions. In other words, "taking seriously" in the context of studies of far-right and/or conspiratorial politics means understanding users as caught up in a complex, fluctuating process of real-making, instead of as "just trolling" (Devries 2021). This framework allows us to bypass a generalizing diagnosis of what causes supposedly homogenous "irrational" belief and to instead focus on what processes of real-making enable alternative worlds to be brought into experiential existence for adherents in the first place.

Christianity and Far-Right Conspiracy

So far, I have drawn from studies of belief and Christianity to present my approach to studying far-right and conspiratorial belief. While this approach is in part driven by the research advantages it affords, drawing from studies of Christianity, belief, and real-making is also necessary for far-right scholars given the ideological and ontological overlap between evangelical Christianity and far-right conspiracies. As I detail below, the shape and function of the contemporary conspiratorial far-right is owed to its coevolution with the cultural dominance of biblically literalist Christianity and its fusion to the mainstream right. It is thus unsurprising that Christian nationalism is set to completely overtake the alt-right as the most prominent far-right threat to democracy and equality within the next several years (Barrón-López 2022), thereby necessitating our engagement with theorizations of belief and material relations.

Throughout the mid to late twentieth century, there was an active combined effort between evangelical lobbyist groups (e.g. the National Association of Evangelicals) and Republican Party strategists to mark the GOP as *the* party of the evangelical voting block—a party that "good" Christians would have no choice but to vote for in order to honor their biblical convictions and religious identity (Williams 2010; Stewart 2020; Butler 2021). The GOP adopted strict adherence to the evangelical Christian vision of moral politics, as this would unite the entire protestant voting block from the U.S. North to the South, whose votes had previously been divided by support or rejection of segregation laws (Butler 2021; Moore 2021; Stewart 2020). During this time, evangelicalism evolved into a trans-denominational movement marked by its biblical literalism, the charismatic tradition (i.e., modern-day miracles and speaking in tongues), a cheerful and color-blind (Bonilla-Silva 2018) opposition to any progressive policy on the basis that America was losing its Christian moorings and needed to return to a Bible-based moral code, and most importantly, a fierce conviction to satisfy religious morals with political reform (Butler 2021).

By the 2000s, the Republican Party had married itself to the Evangelical interpretation of the world, which was as much a political marriage as it was a spiritual and metaphysical one. In 2008, Republican presidential candidate John McCain was obliged to choose a strongly conservative evangelical and young-earth creationist distrustful of mainline science, Sarah Palin, as his vice presidential running mate. This tactic was repeated successfully with President Trump's selection of Vice President Mike Pence, who executes a doctrinal approach to governance from marriage rights to end times–informed foreign policy regarding Israel and Iran (Scahill 2016; Abusalim 2018; Coppins 2018; Farley 2020). Pence's record of biblical values and literalism proved an essential tool for linking Trump's brash character traits and tendency for secular, economically protectionist far-right politics to white evangelicals' desire to establish a nation governed by Christian morality and shaped by biblical-literalist teaching. As of 2021, this means that the mainstream right has not only adopted the traditionalist cultural politics of contemporary evangelical Christianity but also affirms its ontology, that is, its metaphysical interpretation of the world as one that involves powerful invisible actors and spiritual warfare between good and evil. This strategy worked: white evangelical support has become the most reliable Republican voting block (Duin 2021; Cox and Jones 2016; Williams 2010).

This history points to how mainstream Republican politics have become inextricably linked to evangelical ontologies that bolster suspicion of secular science and affirm that invisible, powerful actors are at war in the same physical-spiritual world that everyday Americans occupy. This has afforded friendliness within the Republican party toward extraordinary or otherwise conspiratorial claims that involve unknowable "global elites," dire warfare between good and evil, and an impending apocalyptic or at least government-collapsing event. This is visible in the widespread mistrust that both evangelical and nonevangelical Republicans have in the accuracy of the 2020 American presidential election results, and in the extent that adherents are willing to organize and act on these convictions. Only one third of Republicans express confidence that President Biden won the election fairly; 75 percent of white evangelicals and 54 percent of nonevangelical Republicans agree with the statement that Biden was not legitimately elected (Cox 2021). More alarmingly, 67 percent of white evangelical Republicans and 52 percent of nonevangelical Republicans agree with the statement that an unelected group of government officials known as the "deep state" were working against the interests of the Trump administration in the 2020 election and before. Furthermore, 31 percent of white evangelical Republicans and 25 percent of nonevangelical Republicans agree that "Donald Trump has been secretly fighting a group of child sex traffickers that include prominent Democrats and Hollywood elites" (Cox 2021). As of March 2020, 49 percent of regularly attending white Protestant church goers believe that President Trump was anointed by God to save America, up from 29 percent in 2016 (Berry 2020). When one already affirms the existence of invisible/spiritual actors in the physical world, it is easy to add more (such as global elites) to the bunch.

On January 6, 2021, an estimated eight-hundred people acted on these conspiratorial convictions and descended upon the U.S. Capital buildings in order to halt the presidential inauguration of Democrat Joe Biden. Many were convinced that their action was necessary resistance to the deep state and other invisible, evil forces that were attempting to steal a God-ordained second term from President Donald Trump. Demographic research on the more than seven hundred individuals arrested for breaching the capital indicates that they represent a new kind of violent far-right conspiratorial force, composed mostly (89 percent of those arrested) of "normal," middle class, and middle-aged people who had no obvious ties to traditional fringe far-right groups or organizations (Pape and Ruby 2021). Rather than mobilized by the tactics of traditional far-right organizations, participants engaged in political action because God sent them to engage in spiritual warfare and aid in the fight against the literal demonic forces that supported Democrats (Manseau 2021).

Damon Berry (2020, 71) calls this growing group "prophecy voters," who support Trump in order to perform obedience to prophesies about Trump's divine appointment and the accompanying mandate to combat demonic forces, including the "Marxist," "deep state" and "fake news." To those who occupy this world, "Christians must engage in spiritual warfare and political activism to combat the spiritually malevolent, unpatriotic forces opposing Trump"

(Berry 2020, 72). This literalist combination of the spiritual and the physically present political world is increasingly mainstream within evangelical circles. It is professed in churches (Gilbert 2021), in books from prominent televangelists (see e.g., Evans 2020; Jeremiah 2019), and has even produced grassroots prophets who provide predictions about Trump and the deep state (Duin, 2021), such as the YouTube channel *Ark of Grace* ministries. Ark of Grace streams videos reading out messages received from God and marks important calendar dates for Trump's victory or other events of spiritual warfare.

Perhaps the most infamous contemporary prophet in terms of far-right conspiracy is Q of the QAnon conspiracy. With international followers, QAnon combines traditional far-right antiglobalist (anti-Semitic) content and adoration for contemporary far-right political figures, most notably President Trump, with key features of Christian millennialism. These millennialist features include invisible spiritual battles between forces of good and evil, typically expressed as the belief that Trump's return to presidential office will usher in an end-of-days return of Jesus via the defeat of satanic globalists and the strengthening of God's will on earth (Berry 2020, 77).[1] Other Christian millennialist features of QAnon include anticipation for resurrections of the dead (Kvetenadze 2021), and for the emergence of a one-world government and the roll out of the "mark of the beast" (most recently, the mark is often envisioned as the Covid-19 vaccine). Given these overlaps, it is unsurprising that the QAnon conspiracy theory spreads so easily in Christian churches and communities that prophesy a literal second coming of Christ (Kaleem 2021). As aptly put by Ed Stetzer, evangelical and executive director of the Billy Graham Center, "People of faith believe there is a divine plan—that there are forces of good and forces of evil at work in the world . . . QAnon is a train that runs on the tracks that religion has already put in place" (Rogers 2021).

All considered, when analyzing the contemporary far-right's conspiratorial arm, it is critical to account for how there is now little meaningful distinction between how contemporary right-wing evangelical Christians and far-right conspiratorial prophecy voters come to interpret what is real and true. This merger of the Christian right and far-right conspiracy is largely because of the Republican party's embrace of biblically literalist evangelical Christianity, which shares ontological features with conspiracy: belief in the physical existence and agency of invisible others, spiritual warfare, and a coming great event marking the downfall of evil where a holy figure will judge the wicked. Thus, contemporary study of how far-right conspiratorial beliefs become real to people should attend to the fact that such spiritual and political worlds are inseparable, and thus their felt-realness is produced by the same processual mechanics of belief. In what follows, I attempt this call by applying the theoretical concepts developed here to images that became ethnographic entry points to this political-spiritual world.

Making Contact

The model of belief-as-process described earlier proposes that engagement with material content repeatedly and over time can help make a belief feel real in an embodied way. During these interactions, adherents encounter features of their belief with their senses via material content, digital or otherwise, and thus continue to act in relation to the imminent or potential presence of the actors who populate the belief-system. In other words, embodied experiences with belief materialized via various mediums can play a critical role in what motivates embodied action and subsequently, stronger conviction in the felt presence and agency of gods and monsters (Baker 2011). In what follows, I ground these theoretical conclusions by contextualizing my own interactions with images that materialized belief with the experiences of other ethnographers. I argue that all of these experiences entail encounters with "ontological boundary images."

Unexpected Encounters

Ontological boundary images emerged at various moments during my time spent pursuing ethnographic immersion within various right-wing and conspiratorial public pages on Facebook and Parler, a social media space where conservatives grown tired of Facebook's "censoring" have migrated. Over a period of several months, I spent several hours every other day on these sites. These sites were chosen because their content and user practice often demonstrates the merging of mainstream Christian Right and Republican online practice with contemporary far-right conspiracy as described in part one.[2] This fieldwork entailed several lifestyle changes: it meant a tough commitment to immersing myself with conservative, far-right, and Christian nationalist content in spaces that afford what is sometimes a monotonous scrolling, clicking, and socializing process. This strategy juxtaposed mundane everyday interaction with somewhat fantastical far-right and conspiratorial worlds online. Throughout my months scrolling through these sites, collecting images, and taking field notes, I allowed myself to inhabit the contradiction that is often characteristic of anthropological work. I was both curious about the content encountered while simultaneously skeptical and critical of its claims. Nevertheless, I sought to embody the lifeworld of the far-right local; I read through comment sections, followed links like passageways to sites like Rumble and Bitchute, took in the language, and registered expressions of joy, mutual support, and righteous anger.

The result from assuming this ethnographic position was a heightened sensitivity to when an image sparked a moment of real-making. These moments were defined by when the alternative world proposed by the content felt slightly more tangible than before, and where my own worldview seemed less sturdy. As time passed, I realized this heightened sensitivity wasn't something confined to online spaces; it wasn't something I consciously turned "on" or "off." Rather, the practice of ethnography involves settling into and taking up residence in a field site, allowing the subjects, objects, images, environments, and social systems it contains to bump into and shape the ethnographer in ways they can't yet predict but must respond to. This important hallmark of ethnography is described as "being there," a term that captures how deeply the ethnographer's life must become saturated with the life qualities of the alternative world to which they seek entry (Daynes and Williams 2018; Ingold 2018). For me, consistently living amongst these online images shaped my sensibility to other apocalyptic media in the offline world, which then contributed to my ethnographic experience. Conceptualizing the field site as not bounded by a designated space (see also Desmond 2014) online or offline helped reveal that real-making interactions do not always emerge from dramatic encounters with intentionally designed recruitment content, nor do they always leave someone with a changed mind exactly. Instead, my experiences suggest that conspiratorial beliefs are often nudged into existence when images recurrently and unexpectedly offer up traces of conspiratorial alternative worlds amid everyday life.

For example, during my time spent with far-right images and comment sections, I started cataloging the packages and pamphlets that arrived in the mail, sent my way by a concerned interlocutor who held Christian nationalist beliefs. My interlocutor had signed me up to two separate far-right and right-wing evangelical ministries that each produce a sizable amount of literature to mail to subscribers. At times, I received full books, always hardcover and weighty. As a dutiful ethnographer, I kept these materials nearby, which then began piling up around and under my desk. As time went on, I found that the physical presence of these books, pamphlets, newsletters, and donation envelopes in my home and workspace amplified the presence of the conspiratorial world I was working to enter online. These packages mostly came from the ministry of David Jeremiah, one of the premillennialist pastors who sat on Donald Trump's evangelical advisory board for a brief time (Chastain 2021). Often arriving at unexpected moments, the glossy paper images injected my everyday life with reminders of an alternative spiritual and apocalyptic world that endorsed far-right and conspiratorial politics. In many instances, when I was only anticipating my renewed driver's license or pizza coupons in the mail, I

[Figure 2.1]. Various mail received by the author, including an envelope that acts as a boundary image. Property of author.

would run into multiple envelopes printed with vibrant images that declared the signs of the imminent end times (Figure 2.1).

This particular package (Figure 2.1) is intimidating through its visual aesthetics as well as its material weight. Visually, it combines phenomena that range from the empirically concrete to the entirely subjective and invisible/spiritual. Physical world events (the pandemic; events in Jerusalem), vague representations of current politically charged cultural issues ("socialism" and public cries for shared wealth; cancel culture), entirely abstract or spiritually subjective events (economic chaos; apostasy; spiritual famine), and far-right talking points (globalism) are offered as equally present evidence of the realness of the world where such otherworldly events are both imminent and threatening.

Importantly, the package's materiality not only provides a medium for this image and its message, but it makes the message material.

Threats of globalism and economic chaos become something that I have to hide in my jacket when walking past others in my lobby of my apartment building, and that inevitably take up space on my desk and in my life. The image adds onto the physical presence of other texts, especially as I arrive back at my desk and open the envelope to watch several more images spill out from inside. I first encounter a page folded in half that mimics the front cover of the book recently released by David Jeremiah. It presents a rich sunset looming over a straight, empty desert road that leads into the mountains. It is clear that the sun has descended moments prior, leaving the sky full of deep reds and an impending dark night sky. Humanity has reached its sunset era. Over the image an ominous question is printed in large font: "Where do we go from here?" Both image and question make a claim about the fleeting temporality of the current world and the need to act in response to our current position within the "sunset" of human existence on planet Earth. I notice myself feeling a bit anxious; any rapid depletion of time is certainly a relatable concern. Spiritual apocalypse here connects to a vivid reality from my own ontology: the Earth is warming, and as humans we are running out of time to do anything about it. Inevitably, this shared reality allows the image to resonate just a bit more.

Also included in this package is a large fold-out of the eight signs of the end times printed in colors just as saturated as the envelope, a large bookmark, a page depicting other book packages to be ordered, and an envelope for mailing Jeremiah your donation. All of these prompt purchasing action in response to the eight signs, which are clearly visible in the fold-out image, if not immediately so in the physical world. As I sit with this newly unwrapped content, I glance over at the heavy paperback book that another interlocutor had handed me months earlier, titled *Tipping Point*. It now sits atop a different gifted book, Jeremiah's (2019) *The Book of Signs*. On the inside of *Tipping Point*'s (Evans 2020) cover is a personal message from the gifter, written in big blue pen marks of affectionate swirling cursive. The message ends with "Love and blessings,"

[Figure 2.2]. Collection of materials taking up space in everyday life. Property of author.

highlighted with yellow marker. On the outside cover, an image of the Earth bursting into flames stares back at me. I glanced back to the mail that had somehow spread all over my desk, surrounding these books like a colorful collage. In that moment, I felt the pressure of the physicality of all these messages (Figure 2.2). The first sentence on the pamphlet page with the prophet's image catches my eye to suggest: "You might be living in the last days."

In these moments of encounter with physical images and objects, the ethnographer is placed in an odd position. At once they are suspended between two worlds. First, there is the world experienced by interlocutors, evoked by these pamphlets, books, words, and images. Second, there is the "rational, modern" (Mitchell 2005) world of science and academia that seeks to explain or deconstruct such things, the one that haunts the back of the researcher's brain or looms from their office bookshelves, coloring their responses and offering up theories about what we encounter in the field. The researcher's suspension creates a hybridized ontological position that draws from both worlds; it is a position often referred to as the emic/etic perspective (Jorion 1983). Here, boundaries are porous, and there can emerge a weird sense of doubt in one's own epistemology (Bubandt 2014). From my position as secular ethnographer, it is easy to recognize the similarity this content has to far-right conspiracies, to racist and misogynist interpretations of the world, and evangelical claims of rapture and Armageddon initiated by God and afforded by evil secular elites that have polluted "the culture." Yet, the repetitive and prominent presence of so many texts and images, which also seem to affirm the confidence of my interlocutors, is enough to overwhelm, and I notice more anxious flickers of insecurity in my own secular academic epistemology flutter to the surface of my consciousness, if only for small moments. "They really are invested in this," I hear my mind mention. Later, outside of work hours, I find myself laughing nervously when a friend at a party brings up how microchips can now be implanted into the flesh between thumb and index finger to open your car door. Images from the end-times pamphlet flash through my mind for just a few seconds, and an unconscious thought catches my attention: "Perhaps these are the last days . . ."

Ontological Boundary Images

Such moments of ontological uncertainty, where ethnographers find themselves feeling unexpected emotions, thinking thoughts that contradict their understanding of the world, or even sensing invisible beings are fairly common in both Western and non-Western research contexts. For example, Jessica Johnson (2017) recounts an interaction with a video published by Pastor Mark Driscoll wherein he attempts to smooth over a controversy surrounding his ministry. To her surprise, Johnson finds herself filled with a sense of betrayal at Driscoll's actions, and hopeful that Driscoll would repent of his sins in the video. When Driscoll tells a blatant set of lies instead, she feels an agitation build up in her body, and begins to doubt her senses. Expecting some remorse from Driscoll but finding none, she wonders if she had misheard the video, like I had worried about whether I had been too confident in my own beliefs in the midst of these books and fliers. Johnson considers these moments as irrational, given that she was not and had never been a Christian and/or member of Driscoll's church, and never considered herself as a patron of his pastoral authority. Why should she find herself so bothered by this video and Driscoll's choices? Wasn't she a rational scholar?

In another instance, Susan Harding (1987) famously describes how she felt the world had shifted in some uncanny way after having a long and intensive interview with a Baptist pastor. Driving away after their meeting, she nearly gets into a car accident. In the seconds following the harrowing moment, the thought floats into her mind: "What is God trying to tell me?" She describes this as a moment of coming under conviction, where the pastor's fundamentalist rhetoric filled her mind, turning it into a liminal and contested terrain. Here, boundaries between physical and spiritual worlds are blurred and crossed, if even momentarily during the adrenaline-filled moments of a near miss (Harding 1987). Similarly, after many long days of engaging the practices that her pagan interlocutors used to heighten their imaginative capacities, Tanya Luhrmann (2012) saw three druid figures standing outside her window. She recounts the moment as one that was felt through her senses. The figures appeared just as "real" and tangible as the other objects in her apartment. Thousands of miles away, anthropologist Nils Bubandt (2014) lay alone in a hut bordering swampland in Indonesia, where witches that eat your insides called *gua* are said to congregate. Bubandt hears a gnawing sound outside the hut that he assumes is a dog, before realizing the sound is coming from the roof, where gua are said to perch before leaping onto victims to rip out their insides. He searches for the source of the sound but finds neither dog nor witch. Here, like the absence of the Second Coming after a bout of rapture anxiety, the absence of the source of the sound despite its audible tangibility turns skeptical denial of the existence of witches into uncertainty, doubt in one's own physical and ontological security. As with Harding's (1987) and Johnson's (2017) accounts, this moment of doubt is embodied for Bubandt when it produces a tingling in his spine. In these embodied moments, interactions with videos, texts, sounds, and unfamiliar settings materialize an ambiguous presence, and these presences became real in a way that, as Bubandt (2014, xii) says, "all my doubts about its reality could not dispel."

These authors define such moments in different ways: as encountering surplus affect (Johnson 2017), as coming under conviction (Harding 1987; Johnson 2017), the product of a practiced capacity for imaginative absorption (Luhrmann 2012), entrance into a liminal state where the very terms of physical existence seem to alter (Harding 1987; Bubandt 2014), or as moments of real-making (Luhrmann 2020). If not by their terminology, these accounts are linked in their shared capture of the instability of worlds and their ontological boundaries. In these moments, we get a glimpse of the fact that conversion is not a linear, singular event accomplished through ideational means. Rather, one's mind is changed at various paces, as conviction emerges recurrently through fleeting, embodied events induced by interaction with various materials, whether videos, cars, preachers, books, roofs, sights, sounds, or landscapes.

Susan Leigh Star (1989; 2010) refers to any thing, theory, concept, entity, or other type of object that can be shared or used between different communities as a boundary object. Different communities and positionalities each hold their own representation, understanding, or normative practices with that object. Given its shared use, the boundary object acts as a link between otherwise disparate groups, or as Star (1989) has called them, social worlds. Nick J. Fox (2011) later defined boundary objects as enhancing the capacity of an idea, theory, or practice to translate or travel across culturally defined boundaries. In this sense, boundary objects perform an infrastructural role within social networks, affording connection between individuals from different social worlds via their shared interaction with that object.

In our introduction, we (the authors of this book) defined the boundary image as a particular kind of boundary object. In line with both new materialists and critiques of affective versus textual dualism, we recognize the vibrance of images by marking them as assemblages composed of interacting materials and technologies like code and screens, affective charges, and semantics charged with historical and cultural weight. We understand images to carry the same materiality as any object (especially digital images that otherwise seem immaterial) but also to carry distinct capacities for representation, language, and to thus have their own form of agency. Images "are like living organisms" that have and communicate desires as well as lives (Mitchell 2005, 11). Boundary images, then, are those lively representations that act as connection modules between entities.

The items from the mail are certainly lively images, representations of imminent but momentarily absent phenomena (sunsets, dry deserts, not-yet-purchased book bundles) built with various materials (ink, paper, histories, and symbols). At the same time, the features of those images, both material and symbolic, offer an interaction wherein the borders between one ontology (that of the researcher) and another (that of the believer) are blurred. These images were the infrastructure necessary to make me, if only for a moment, doubt my ontological stability. Given the role of these images within these embodied moments of border crossing between *worlds,* we should think of these materials not just as boundary images, but as *ontological* boundary images (OBIs). In other words, boundary images that are involved in interactions that become real-making moments can be distinguished with the term ontological boundary images. OBIs are the stuff that facilitate moments of real-making.

To qualify an image as an ontological boundary image (as opposed to just a boundary image) can therefore signal that representations—i.e., abstract or symbolic imagery alongside the material features that carry the image (paper, ink, pixels, computer monitors, or bits of code)—are active within real-making interactions within a given moment. Any image has the capacity to be a boundary image, just as any object has the capacity to function as a boundary object when it facilitates connections between otherwise disparate nodes in a social or technological network (Star 2010). Similarly, any boundary image has the capacity to become an ontological boundary image if it were to include or provide the multifaceted infrastructure necessary to induce a moment of real-making. However, the image's capacity to do any of this depends on the other actors involved in the interaction and the histories involved in the relation (Powell 2013). Inevitably, conspiratorial, religious, and/or far-right images are encountered differently by interlocutor, researcher, and outsider, given their unresolvable social positionalities. It is important to emphasize that one's whiteness, one's history of being raised within religious or secular worldviews, and one's social and educational class all affect whether an image will function as an ontological boundary image (Frankenburg 1993; Hill-Collins 2004; Haraway 2004; Smith 1974).

Ethnographic "closeness" is thus crucial to the study of ontological boundary images and moments of real-making. For the average observer, these mail fliers I received and their warnings about Armageddon might understandably seem absurd, creepy, or as cheap sales ploys (interpretations indeed expressed by folks outside of my research). However, for the ethnographer who cultivates a suspended emic/etic position, these encounters facilitate moments wherein the alternative world becomes tangible and real, if fleetingly. Analysis of this specific phenomena via attention to when images become ontological boundary images activates the ethnographer's emic/etic perspective as a source of data in itself (Chiseri-Strater 1996; Bounegru, Devries, and Weltevrede 2022). Put another way, attention to OBIs is an epistemological strategy for highlighting the microprocesses that cultivate spiritual and/or conspiratorial conviction in ways that are deeply relational and that involve the agency of human participants, digital and analogue materiality, histories, and symbolic representations. In this sense, attention to ontological boundary images allows us to prioritize study of the world-building relations that emerge not only during the image's interactions with humans but also with religion and political histories.

Doubt and the Globalists

In this section, I describe encounters that I had with boundary images during my time cultivating an emic/etic perspective online, which was punctuated by the packages I received in the mail. My attention to the interactions that I had with these media is in part informed by Giddings's (2009) concept of microethnography, which pushes ethnographers to consider media objects and their technological features as part(icipants) in shaping the outcome of a dynamic, relational encounter. Giddings (2009) remarks that it is in these microencounters with bits of media or technologies that cultural experiences are produced. Considering digital features as actively involved in the formation of cultural experience helps provide an explanation for how online landscapes come to feel either foreign, familiar, trustworthy, or compelling. Facebook is a hyperfamiliar space, but as an ethnographer scrolling through far-right or conspiratorial pages and posts, I was often left unsettled either by the extremeness or the ambiguity of some of the content encountered, whether in the form of images or the comment discussions that framed these images.

In these moments, bits of code and other data materialize images and community discussion surrounding far-right conspiratorial worlds, providing a series of interactive opportunities for the user. As mentioned, the output of these opportunities as real-making interactions is dependent on the variety of other ingredients the user brings to the table: familiarity with the content, how often such phrases expressed online might actually be used within their offline engagements with family and friends, and so on (Giddings 2009). In my case, I am driven to interact both by the deep curiosity of any ethnographer, and what often feels like a need to dig deeper into a post in order to understand what exactly is going on. In one instance, I find myself scrolling through a Facebook page called

"The Trump Revolution," still active with daily posts as of late 2021. Many of the images on the page are shared from personal Facebook profiles, suggesting a reliable network of individual users (not groups or pages) who have made their personal Facebook profile public and available to be sourced for images. Intrigued by these users' dedication to use their personal Facebook pages for political ends, I click on one user's profile whose images had been shared several times within The Trump Revolution. Scrolling through the content posted by this user, I came across a mysterious looking thumbnail and video link. Clicking the link, I am anxiously transported to Bitchute, an alt-tech video-hosting service that, like other far-right alt-tech, describes itself as offering "freedom of expression."[3] I allowed my emotions of intrigue and confusion to come forward in my mind as the video began to play, presenting a grainy, dark image of a bearded white man in an all-black suit, sitting at a desk. The background seems industrial, and in the foreground a microphone sits in front of the man's folded hands. It is a scene more reminiscent of the film *V for Vendetta* (2005) than from a contemporary YouTuber or influencer. A bright red and yellow icon reading "War-Room" at the bottom right of the screen contrasts the blue, black, and gray aesthetic of the figure and his surroundings. The image is meant to be both theatrical and deeply serious, and it somehow successfully captures these contradictions among the weird digital space of Bitchute.

The video moves to stories of voter fraud, presenting a narrative through images of supposedly hacked voting machines. I feel myself dismissive of these claims of voter fraud, but I am simultaneously struck by the fact that I didn't have an immediate set of resources available to debunk the very specific evidence the video presented for voting-machine manipulation. Like Bubandt (2014) and the gua, a part of me knows that in that moment I lack material evidence to entirely disprove the existence of these faulty machines, and I feel compromised in my opposition. As the narrative goes on, the video presents images of George Soros and the Clintons, implying that even mundane images of them standing or walking around in the world are evidence of their evil. The images shift again to show grainy footage of Soros smiling and waving on a balcony. The footage gradually zooms in, and finally pauses on Soros's face as it seems to contort into an unnatural, evil grin while ominous music plays.

In any other setting, perhaps when a friend shares a conspiracy video they found casually scrolling online as a joke, the absurd attempted seriousness of this video might induce laughter, or the assumption that these people are simply crazy. Instead, alone in the ethnographic setting and surrounded by an unfamiliar platform, my body becomes conflicted with various forms of disgust; I immediately recognize the historic antisemitic dog whistles and the subtle implication that some supernatural evil is affiliated with or acting through unknowable (Jewish) elites like Soros (see Hanebrink 2018). The intensity of the conspiratorial claim itself strikes me as seriously dark and connected to past and contemporary human suffering. The problem, however, is that I notice myself responding not just to the fascistic darkness designing this narrative but simultaneously to the affective darkness and graveness the video means to convey: an unknowable evil collection of power captured in images of Soros's face, intermittently narrated by a mysterious *V for Vendetta*–like figure in black. I feel as if I am interacting with illicit knowledge, something the rest of the world doesn't know about.

While I know in my logical mind that these claims are false and dangerous, this cognitive assurance is not enough to prevent an illogical slippage from the sturdiness of my own world into a liminal and nonsturdy reality, wherein monsters like these may exist. Indeed, billionaires (not Jewish people) do reek havoc on the world (Mayer 2017). As Ahmed (2004) writes and others affirm (Johnson 2017; Stewart 2007), affect is relational, emerging not from individual bodies but from the coming together of various actors. Affect is here generated by the various microinteractions between myself as ethnographer and the features of the video, the platform that hosts it, and the network of links and connections that brought me here, producing a series of contradictions and speculations I cannot immediately dispel. I again feel the tickling of what I know to be an irrational thought in the back of my mind: "what if something is going on with voting machines?"

After closing the browsers and leaving my computer, my body is left feeling unsettled from my interactions with these monsters, even though they were "merely" mediated images and even though I recognize them as fictions of anti-Semitic far-right conspiracy that for a century have had violent consequences. I'd stepped back into my own reality, and yet I am marked by the otherworldly interaction. While this moment will have no lasting effect on the ontology I inhabit, the interaction shows how video images nevertheless have the capacity to evoke ontological uncertainty, thus qualifying them as ontological boundary images that help create what actual adherents experience as the undeniable tangibility of an alternative world, where such monsters are active. This indicates that recurrent contact with such forms evokes the possible presence of monsters and mass deception, a presence that adherents and sometimes anthropologists experience in an embodied way.

Playing with Monsters

The images from the video discussed above materialize conspiratorial belief in a way that takes itself seriously. Despite how cheesy the video may look to outsiders, it is clear that the intention is to evoke the imminent presence of such globalist monsters so that viewers experience concern, anger, or feel motivated to pursue more secret, supposedly suppressed knowledge about the world they inhabit. The images in this next encounter, on the other hand, take a different approach. Instead of taking an hour to present evidence or make explicit claims about the world, these images present a brief dramatic enactment. In October 2020, a young woman uploaded a TikTok meant to draw parallels between government mandates for Covid-19 vaccines and what the imagined "roll out" of the mark of the beast would be like in the biblical end times. In the forty-second video, the sole actor, the young white woman, depicts herself being beaten to death by government authorities for not taking the Covid-19 vaccine, as is taught will happen to believers who refuse the mark of the beast during the prophesied biblical end times (e.g. see Jeremiah 2019). Given the intense approach taken by this narrative, the TikTok rapidly went viral within liberal and progressive communities online. While the video was soon deleted, many users duetted[4] the video to point out the absurdity in such a comparison, as well as the uncomfortable vividness with which the young woman enacts her martyrdom. As one user put it, "White women are so DRAMATIC!" These reworks serve not only as a necessary call-out of the trope of white women's victimhood (historically and contemporarily used to justify racist violence) but also as a reminder that Christian nationalists see reality quite differently than the rest of us.

Not meaning to interact with research content at the time, I first discovered this particular video while scrolling through my personal TikTok, where I encountered one of the various duets a progressive user had made that showed only a brief snapshot of the original TikTok. Despite the brevity of the encounter, the contemporary apocalypticism and mainstream aesthetic of the young woman in the original TikTok intrigued me as an ethnographer, given especially that I was conducting the previously discussed fieldwork at the time. I sought out the full version and settled in for what dystopian affects the images might offer up.

The images in the TikTok shift quickly; all dialogue is presented through text on screen while a slowed, emotional pop ballad plays. The first words I register are "I'm not ready to die, not yet," from the song. The text on screen shows the young woman saying she's "not ready to die yet," and that she will take the vaccine. She holds out her arm, and the words **chip implanted** appear on the screen, which is when I quickly recognize that this is both a video about Covid-19 vaccines *and* the tribulation period leading up to the second coming of Christ. By depicting the vaccine as a microchip (a microchip is how many evangelicals predict the mark of the beast will materialize, e.g. see Jeremiah 2019), the moving images create a tangible link between the observable world wherein Covid-19 vaccines exist and an alternative one where Christ's second coming and the violent persecution of Christians is imminent. The images propose that this world is already revealed in government mandates like vaccines that we can see and experience in "real life." Like the envelope I received, these moving images positioned invisible spiritual events alongside vividly tangible ones (vaccine mandates) becoming OBIs in the process.

The video then shows a different white woman (played by the same woman). Contrasting the first woman who took the vaccine, this character wears a red ball cap reminiscent but not identical to Trump's infamous "Make America Great Again" hat. In this, the character's image provides another instance where tangible, observable-world objects like the MAGA hat come into contact with figures from alternative worlds. She looks upward and offscreen toward where we assume an invisible authority figure stands above her. Via the onscreen text, the invisible figure asks her if she will take the vaccine. She refuses, only to be told that she will be killed for such a choice. Looking fearful, she responds with "I know" and is depicted as being "taken away" by the invisible figure. I then watch her recoil as dark-red fake blood and black eyes appear on her tear-stained face. The invisible figure tells her she can still refuse, to which she avidly refuses while smiling up at the figure with her stained-red face, only to be "beaten" further.

Apart from these disturbing visuals, I feel bombarded by the paired music: the emotional pop ballad now evokes the musical aesthetic of Christian worship music. The music is dramatic and pleading, the chord progressions designed to make the hairs on your arms raise regardless of your religiousness. The character recoils and shudders, her blackened eyes close, and more blood appears as she seems to sing along to the reverb-filled song. The vocals swell and declare: "I'm down on my knees and I need you to be my God, be my help, be my savior . . ." Just as the word *saviour* is sung, I watch as the woman is then depicted as an angel in heaven. God's words pulled from Bible verses now appear on screen "Well done good and faithful servant," stating God's satisfaction with the *political* loyalty and martyrdom of his "faithful servant."

While watching, I feel my emotions build into a gross tangle. I am made uncomfortable by the young woman's overly dramatic depiction of blood and violence, as well as the assertion that God needs suffering martyrs. I am disturbed because of the historic harm caused by white women alleging persecution by "others" (especially by people of color), and also by the juxtaposition of the message's intensity with the obvious fakeness of the narrative and the scene itself, which is filmed in the young woman's home. Most obviously disturbing is the surface message: that there will come a point where nonvaccinated individuals will be murdered by their governments—a victim narrative entirely absent from the actual racialized reality of the United States' prison industrial complex and death row (Alexander 2010). Given this misplaced victimhood and exaggeration, it is somewhat unsurprising that the video went viral via left-wing accounts and journalists sharing the video to (rightly) call out the harm caused by videos that equate receiving a vaccine either to death, harm, or a loss in some political-spiritual battle. In some contradiction, to outsiders the video seemed both like intentional disinformation (information spread with an active intent to deceive) and also a depiction of what all right-wing groups *must* objectively believe (e.g., Craker 2020): that left-wing governments are monstrous killers of Christians, propelled by agency of Satan.

In the midst of this, I find myself wondering, do folks actually take this seriously? For how long? Does any viewer who supports or enjoys this video really see it as a literal depiction of current events? Still perplexed, I go to the TikTok profile of the user who created the video in order to check for similar videos she may have made and to read the comment sections. My ethnographic observations elsewhere (Devries 2022) attest that users who post extreme far-right or explicitly conspiratorial content on Facebook tend to post such content a majority of the time. However, this was not the case with the user who created this video. Instead, her content generally worked to beautify the lifestyle of a young, traditional, conservative, pro-Trump Christian white woman. Christian themes like purity culture and trusting God emerge alongside mainstream traditionalist politics (pro-gun, anti-BLM, heteronormative messages). The comment sections were equally a representation of mundane, conservative Christian life; most complimented the creator's makeup, asked for hair or makeup tutorials, or left otherwise uplifting and unassuming comments.

To me, this affirmed that the video was a playful, semi-serious enactment of still deeply felt belief about the persecution of Christians and Republicans and the imminence of the end times, as opposed to something created with the active intent to recruit or mobilize political movement, as the video with Soros might be. Notably, the video is tagged as using the "POV" (point-of-view) style, a format on TikTok where the content creator depicts an archetypal scene that hasn't necessarily happened but provides entertainment and resonates with viewers in its relatability. In cases like these, showing the vaccine as mark of the beast, the violence of invisible, not-*yet*-present government authorities, or even the claim that the user would die for their beliefs presents a playful exercise in using observable world objects (like vaccines and Trump hats) to depict (monstrous) political possibilities. Viewers' interactions with images that depict vaccines and Trump supporters (tangible things) combined with biblical prophecies (intangible things) affords a bridging between those tangible and intangible worlds. Here, the reality that there are Christians out there who are or will be oppressed for refusing the Covid-19 vaccine becomes tangible despite its absence (Baker 2011). In this way, even images not intended to convert or mobilize act as ontological boundary images, since interactions with dramatized images contribute to an embodied experience of living in a world where such threats *could* materialize at any second.

As Massumi (2015) writes in "The Future Birth of the Affective Fact," the threat that monsters or other harms that various rhetorics depict could emerge in the future is often more generative of belief and subsequent action than evidence for their nonexistence. Massumi describes such affective politics as operating through a logic of preemption that both becomes self-causing and hinges on the conditional. Discussing George W. Bush's reference to Iraq's nonexistent weapons of mass destruction, Massumi explains how even if a threat (e.g. Iraq's WMD) does not eventuate into actual danger, the feeling that such an enemy "could have" produced danger remains. It is this "could" that motivated and provided logics of support for "precautionary" offensive actions toward Iraq.

This brings us to an alarming point that further highlights the need to analyze alternative worlds that folks inhabit, where threats from foreign or satanic others are deeply felt as imminent. Preemptive action in response to the potential threat will always be justifiable to adherents regardless of whether that threat is manifested only through rhetoric or imagery and never becomes present. This is because, in Massumi's terms, an "affective fact" has already been produced: that there exists an imminent (if not quite present) threat, and subsequent actions (whether violent or precautionary ones) should thus be carried out. Massumi calls this process "ontopower": power that works through ontological experience but is dependent on virtual representations. In the midst of a resurgent wave of Christian nationalism in the United States, we should consider OBIs like this TikTok to deliver a kind of mundane ontopower that reflects the growing hegemony of evangelical institutions. Dangerously, these OBIs both playfully materialize an alternative conspiratorial world but also subtly evoke the possible realness of an impending spiritual threat within the quotidian setting of a homemade TikTok. Here, we encounter a functional contradiction, where ontological boundary imagery connects the worlds of digital play and spiritual warfare.

As we have seen, monstrous depictions of what is *possible* but not necessarily what *is* are common in both right-wing politics, as in Bush's war, and in far-right conspiratorial imagery. In the case of the TikTok, this imagery can be somewhat playful in its obvious

[Figure 2.3]. Lizard man presents possible imminent evils. Screenshot from video posted to Rumble by user *And We Know*. Title: "This BATTLE is SPIRITUAL! In the END, WE WIN! FURY fight is a GREAT EXAMPLE! PRAY!" Published October 10, 2021.

fakeness, yet it also asks, "what if?" Sometime after watching the TikTok, I found myself watching an hour-long video hosted on Rumble that I had found by scrolling on Parler during fieldwork. Amid the mundanity of my living room, I listened to the video give another account of how powerful elites controlled the roll-out of the Covid-19 vaccine and of how "big" revelations will emerge in the coming weeks. Somewhat suddenly, I am alerted by the image of a scaly, red, lizard man in a suit that fades onto the screen (Figure 2.3). The image is only there for a few seconds, but its intensity revived my senses that had perhaps otherwise been dulled from the length of the overall video. The lizard man (a demon? The devil himself?) is depicted awarding a medal to Dr. Fauci, a government figure in charge of Covid-19 mandates in the United States largely attached to Covid-19 conspiracies by far-right adherents.

The specific content of the image itself may evoke shock, laughter, and disbelief to any viewer, emic or etic. Everyone watching knows this is a doctored image. It evokes a smirk, an embodied response driven from the image's obvious fakeness. However, simultaneously, I notice the potential for viewers to resonate in some affective way with the image. Many far-right adherents experience Fauci as a pawn of evil elites; as an ethnographer, I am also familiar with this alternative world version of Dr. Fauci. When viewers encounter Fauci through their brief interaction with this image, what becomes potent is not the accuracy of the image but its suggestion about what could be true, even if in some other, similar form. Massumi (2015) would say that such images don't produce objective facts but instead affective ones. When encountered, affective facts attest to the potential and therefore imminent realness of worlds that involve such monsters, whether they appear exactly as depicted here or not. For the spiritual-conspiratorial adherent, this affective fact about the state of the world also becomes a tangible, physical fact about the world's actors. It is thus during such an encounter that we can name images like this one as ontological boundary images. Like the others discussed throughout this chapter, the OBI here does not have to be deeply compelling in and of itself. It is not accurate to assume such images immediately convince foolish viewers in a kind of techno-determinist fashion. Rather, OBIs open up avenues for travel, provoking both humor and other affects like worry and uncertainty. It is in paying attention to these complexities and contradictions via the concept of ontological boundary images that we might get closer to understanding how exactly far-right and conspiratorial worlds, over time, become real and threatening.

The Image Medium

In this chapter I have asked how images are involved in processes of far-right and conspiratorial real-making. I have avoided a definition of belief as a stable, coherent epistemology or as an abstract, "irrational" set of conclusions about the actual world. Instead, I have proposed that far-right and conspiratorial adherents consistently build alternative worlds through their embodied interactions with materialized depictions of imminent (if currently absent) monsters, like Satan and globalists, or gods and political saviors. It is interactive contact with those images that materialize belief—ontological boundary images—that enable such deep political conviction (Luhrmann 2012; 2020; Baker 2011).

In a fitting exercise of boundary blurring, I have inserted the media-studies, new materialist (e.g., Allen 2018; Bennet 2010; Coleman 2008) inquiry of "what do images do?" into an anthropological and religious studies framework about belief, and as well into philo-sophical frameworks of what constitutes worldmaking and reality (Goodman 1978; 1984). I have attempted this so that we might differently approach questions about the spread of conspiracy and far-right subjectivity. While there has been a surge in research regarding extreme far-right online communities and digital networks of mis/disinformation, what has remained relatively unstudied is, as Mitchell (2005, 49) puts it, the relationality of image and beholder within the context of the far right. How, exactly, does an image produce conviction in far-right worlds? Where or what is the affective, embodied process that emerges between humans and the content they encounter online (or offline)?

The concept of the ontological boundary image is meant to help shed light on this particular process by marking a temporal moment and ontological process that contributes to and maintains conviction in a given world. In moments where we sit surrounded by images and pamphlets, books, and other literature, or alone in a foreign village at night, we might sense a bridge forming under our feet, indicating the possibility of crossing into a world wherein monsters not yet seen exist. When conditions are right, ontological boundary images achieve this through their material presence and the semiotic content therein, producing gods and monsters whose presence flirts with the physical world. To use Marshall McLuhan's (1964) concept that the medium is the message, here, ontological boundary images are both the message and (psychic) medium to make contact with invisible others and alternative worlds.

As my own ethnographic encounters showcased, interactions with OBIs offer a complex and contradictory experience. OBIs occupy mundane lifestyle tasks (checking the mail), habits, hobbies, and they emerge during everyday practices (scrolling through Facebook, reading spiritual literature, shopping, donating). While deeply quotidian, these interactions can provide an overwhelming engagement with the conspiratorial and the apocalyptic. As a result, prophetic, political, spiritual, and everyday stakes merge to produce a tangible urgency that sometimes compels practical action and further involvement with similar images. From here, we can begin to understand ontological boundary images as lending insight into unsettlingly unassuming processes of far-right recruitment and mobilization, where conspiratorial worlds are not the product of foreign disinformation campaigns but are forged recurrently amid the ingredients of everyday life.

Notes

1   Note that the millennialist doctrine practiced by "prophecy voters" differs from the premillennialism discussed earlier in the text, which asserts that the rapture will occur before events of tribulation. Millennialists believe they will still be on Earth and must fight against events of tribulation, hence their mobilization to participate in spiritual-political warfare.

2   This is as opposed to more fringe websites notorious for their specifically alt-right play and historically antagonistic and atheistic subculture, namely Reddit and 4Chan.

3   Unsurprisingly, Bitchute has thus become what the Anti-Defamation League defines as a "hotbed of hate," platforming conspiracy theorists and other far-right, violent, supremacist content. The ADL refers to Bitchute as a "recruiting ground for extremists" (https://www.adl.org/blog/bitchute-a-hotbed-of-hate).

4   Duetting describes a common practice on TikTok where a user makes their own video that plays alongside a video made previously by another user. The point is typically to make commentary on the original video.

References

Abusalim, Dorgham. 2018. "Messianic Mike Pence Spouts Pseudo-Biblical Literalism in Jerusalem." *Mondoweiss.* Accessed January 5, 2022. https://mondoweiss.net /2018/01/christian-zionist-jerusalem/.

Ahmed, Sara. 2004. "Affective Economies." *Social Text* 22, no. 2: 117–39. https://doi .org/10.1215/01642472-22-2_79-117.

Alexander, Michelle. 2010. *The New Jim Cros: Mass Incarceration in the Age of Color-Blindness.* New York: The New Press.

Allen, Louisa. 2018. "Methodological Matters: The Becoming of Data about Sexuality at School." In *Sexuality Education and New Materialism: Queer Things*. New York: Palgrave MacMillan.

Baker, K. J. 2011. "Getting Rapture Ready: The Materiality of the Rapture in North America." *Studies in World Christianity* 17, no. 2: 101–18. https://doi.org/10.3366/swc.2011.0015.

Barrón-López, Laura. 2022. "Concerns Grow over the Increasing Ties between Christianity and Right-Wing Nationalism." *PBS Newshour*. Accessed December 14, 2022. https://www.pbs.org/newshour/show/concerns-grow-over-the-increasing-ties-between-christianity-and-right-wing-nationalism.

Bennet, J. 2010. *Vibrant Matter: A Political Ecology of Things*. Durham, N.C.: Duke University Press.

Beren, Dale. 2019. *It Came from Something Awful: How a Toxic Troll Army Accidentally Memed Donald Trump into Office*. New York: All Points Books.

Berry, D. 2020. "Voting in the Kingdom." *Nova Religio* 23, no. 4: 69–93.

Bonilla-Silva, Eduardo. 2018. *Racism without Racists: Color-blind Racism and the Persistence of Racial Inequality in America*. Lanham, Md.: Rowman & Littlefield.

Bounegru, L., M. Devries, and E. Weltevrede. 2022. "The Research Persona Method: Figuring and Reconfiguring Personalised Information Flows." In *Figure: Concept and Method*, ed. Scott Wark, Celia Lury, and William Viney, 77–104. New York: Palgrave MacMillan. https://link.springer.com/chapter/10.1007/978-981-19-2476-7_5.

Bubandt, N. 2014. *The Empty Seashell: Witchcraft and Doubt on an Indonesian Island*. Ithaca, N.Y.: Cornell University Press.

Butler, Anthea. 2021. *White Evangelical Racism: The Politics of Morality in America*. Chapel Hill: University of North Carolina Press.

Chastain, Blake. 2021. "Exvangelical Tiktokkers Aren't a Sign of the End Times. But here's What Evangelicals Need to Understand about 'The Falling Away.'" *Religion Dispatches*. Accessed January 13, 2022. https://religiondispatches.org/exvangelical-tiktokkers-arent-a-sign-of-the-end-times-but-heres-what-evangelicals-need-to-understand-about-the-falling-away/.

Chiseri-Strater, Elizabeth. 1996. "Turning in upon Ourselves: Positionality, Subjectivity, and Reflexivity in Case Study and Ethnographic Research." In *Ethics and Representation in Qualitative Studies of Literacy*, ed. Peter Mortensen and Gesa E. Kirsch, 115–33. Urbana, Ill.: National Council of Teachers of English.

Coleman, Rebecca. 2008. "The Becoming of Bodies: Girls, Media Effects, and Body Image." *Feminist Media Studies* 8, no. 2: 163–79. https://doi.org/10.1080/14680770801980547.

Coppins, McKay. 2018. "God's Plan for Mike Pence: Will the Vice President—and the Religious Right—Be Rewarded for Their Embrace of Donald Trump?" *The Atlantic*. Accessed January 5, 2022. https://www.theatlantic.com/magazine/archive/2018/01/gods-plan-for-mike-pence/546569/.

Cox, Daniel A. 2021. "Rise of Conspiracies Reveals an Evangelical Divide in the GOP." *American Survey Center*. Accessed January 5, 2022. https://www.americansurveycenter.org/rise-of-conspiracies-reveal-an-evangelical-divide-in-the-gop/.

Craker, Ezra. 2020. "Popular TikToks Promote Unfounded Claim That COVID-19

Vaccine Could Be the Mark of the Beast." *Chimes*. Accessed November 22, 2021. https://calvinchimes.org/2020/12/03/popular-tiktoks-promote-unfounded-claim -that-covid-19-vaccine-could-be-the-mark-of-the-beast/.

Daynes, Sarah and Terry Williams. 2018. *On Ethnography*. Medford: Polity Press.

Desmond, M. 2014. "Relational Ethnography." *Theory and Society* 43, no. 5: 547–79. https://doi.org/10.1007/s11186-014-9232-5.

Devries, Melody. 2021. "Mobilized but Not (Yet) Recruited: The Case of the Collective Avatar." In *Rise of the Far-Right: Technologies of Recruitment and Mobilization,* ed. M. Devries, J. Bessant, R. Watts. Lanham, Md: Rowman & Littlefield.

Devries, Melody. 2022. "Archetypes and Homophilic Avatars: New Approaches to Studying Far-Right Facebook Practice." *Canadian Journal of Communication* 47, no. 1: 151–71.

Devries, Melody, and Noel Brett. 2021. "Processes of Authentication and 'Fake' News: On Gaining System Access." *Items: Insights from the Social Sciences.* Social Science Research Council. https://mediawell.ssrc.org/news-items/processes-of-authenti cation-and-fake-news-on-gaining-system-access-items/. [July 14, 2021]

Duin, Julia. 2021. "The Christian Prophets Who Say Trump Is Coming Again." *Politico*. Accessed January 5, 2022. https://www.politico.com/news/magazine/2021/02/18/ how-christian-prophets-give-credence-to-trumps-election-fantasies-469598.

Evans, J. 2020. *Tipping Point: The End Is Here*. Dallas, Tex.: XO Publishing.

Farley, Audrey. 2020. "The Apocalyptic Ideas Influencing Pence and Pompeo Could Also Power the Left." *Washington Post.* Accessed January 5, 2022. https://www .washingtonpost.com/outlook/2020/01/28/apocalyptic-ideas-influencing-pence -pompeo-could-also-power-left/.

Fox, Nick J. 2011. "Boundary Objects, Social Meanings and the Success of New Tech-nologies." Sociology 45 (1): 70–85. https://doi.org/10.1177/0038038510387196.

Frankenburg, Ruth. 1993. *White Women, Race Matters: The Social Construction of White-ness.* Minneapolis: University of Minnesota Press.

Giddings, Seth. 2009. "Events and Collusions: A Glossary for the Microethnography of Video Game Play." *Games and Culture* 4, no. 2: 144–57. https://doi.org/10.1177/ 1555412008325485.

Gilbert, David. 2021. "Evangelical Pastors Are Secretly Spreading the Gospel of QAnon on YouTube." *Vice News.* Accessed February 3, 2022. https://www.vice.com/en/ article/m7v75n/qanon-shaman-jan-6-celebration-prison-phone-call.

Goodman, Nelson. 1978. *Ways of Worldmaking*. Indianapolis, Ind.: Hackett Publishing Company.

Goodman, Nelson. 1984. *Of Mind and Other Matters.* Cambridge, Mass.: Harvard University Press.

Hanebrink, Paul. 2018. *A Spectre Haunting Europe: The Myth of Judeo-Bolshevism.* Cam-bridge, Mass.: Harvard University Press.

Haraway, Donna. 2004. "Situated Knowledges." In *The Feminist Standpoint Theory Reader: Intellectual and Political Controversies,* ed. Sandra Harding, 81-101. New York: Routledge.

Harding, S. F. 1987. "Convicted by the Holy Spirit: The Rhetoric of Fundamental Bap-tist Conversion." *American Ethnologist* 14, no. 1: 167–81.

Hartzler, Aaron. 2014. *Rapture Practice: A True Story about Growing Up Gay in an Evangelical Family*. Boston: Little, Brown & Company.

Hebdige, Dick. 1979. *Subcultures: The Meaning of Style.* London: Routledge.

Hill-Collins, Patricia. 2004. "Learning from the Outsider Within: The Sociological Significance of Black Feminist Thought." In *The Feminist Standpoint Theory Reader,* ed. Sandra Harding, 103–26. New York: Routledge, 2004.

Ingold, Tim. 2018. Anthropology: Why It Matters. Medford: Polity Press.

Jeremiah, David. 2019. *The Book of Signs: 31 Undeniable Prophecies of the Apocalypse.* Nashville, Tenn.: W Publishing Group.

Johnson, Jessica. 2017. "Bodily Encounters: Affect, Religion, and Ethnography." In *Feeling Religion,* ed. J. Corrigan, 200–221. Durham, N.C.: Duke University Press.

Jones, R. P. 2016. "Donald Trump and the Transformation of White Evangelicals." *Time*. Accessed January 5, 2022. https://time.com/4577752/donald-trump -transformation-white-evangelicals/.

Jorion, P. 1983. "Emic and Etic: Two Anthropological Ways of Spilling Ink." *Cambridge Anthropology* 8, no. 3: 41–68.

Kaleem, Jaweed. 2021. "QAnon and Other Conspiracy Theories Are Taking Hold in Churches. Pastors Are Fighting Back." *Los Angeles Times*. Accessed January 5, 2022. https://www.latimes.com/world-nation/story/2021-03-03/ la-na-church-qanon-conspiracy-theories.

Kvetenadze, Téa. 2021. "QAnon Believers Gather in Dallas Awaiting Return of Long-Dead JFK Jr." *Forbes*. Accessed November 2, 2021. https://www.forbes.com/sites/ teakvetenadze/2021/11/02/qanon-believers-gather-in-dallas-awaiting-return-of -long-dead-jfk-jr/?sh=47c6a1e8668f.

Luhrmann, Tanya. M. 2012. *When God Talks Back: Understanding the American Evangelical Relationship with God*. New York: Alfred A. Knopf.

Luhrmann, Tanya. 2020. *How God Becomes Real: Kindling the Presence of Invisible Others*. Princeton, N.J.: Princeton University Press.

Manseau, Peter. 2021. "Some Capitol Rioters Believed They Answered God's Call, not Just Trump's." *The Washington Post*. Accessed February 3, 2022. https://www.wash ingtonpost.com/outlook/2021/02/11/christian-religion-insurrection-capitol-trump/.

Massumi, Brian. 2015. "The Future Birth of the Affective Fact: The Political Ontology of Threat." In *Ontopower: War, Powers, and the State of Perception*. Durham, N.C.: Duke University Press.

Mayer, Jane. 2017. *Dark Money: The Hidden History of the Billionaires behind the Rise of the Radical Right.* New York: Anchor.

McLuhan, Marshall. 1964. *Understanding Media: The Extensions of Man.* New York: McGraw-Hill.

McTeigue, James. 2005. *V For Vendetta.* Film. Warner Brothers Pictures.

Miller-Idriss, Cynthia. 2020. *Hate in the Homeland: The New Global Far Right.* Princeton, N.J.: Princeton University Press.

Mitchell, W. J. T. 2005. *What Do Pictures Want? The Lives and Loves of Images.* Chicago: University of Chicago Press.

Moore, Leonard N. 2021. *Teaching Black History to White People.* Austin: University of Texas Press.

Pape, Robert A., and Kevin Ruby. 2021. "The Capitol Rioters Aren't Like Other Extremists." *The Atlantic*. Accessed December 22, 2021. https://www.theatlantic.com/ideas/archive/2021/02/the-capitol-rioters-arent-like-other-extremists/617895/.

Phillips, Whitney. 2015. *This Is Why We Can't Have Nice Things: Mapping the Relationship between Online Trolling and Mainstream Culture*. Cambridge, Mass.: MIT Press.

Powell, Christopher. 2013. "Radical Relationism: A Proposal." In *Conceptualizing Relational Sociology,* eds. Christopher Powell and François Dépelteau, 187–207. New York: Palgrave Macmillan.

Rogers, Kaleigh. 2021. "Why QAnon Has Attracted So Many White Evangelicals." *FiveThirtyEight.* Accessed January 5, 2022. https://fivethirtyeight.com/features/why-qanon-has-attracted-so-many-white-evangelicals/.

Scahill, Jeremy. 2016. "Mike Pence Will Be the Most Powerful Christian Supremacist in U.S. History." *The Intercept.* January 5, 2022. https://theintercept.com/2016/11/15/mike-pence-will-be-the-most-powerful-christian-supremacist-in-us-history/.

Smith, Dorothy. 1974. "Women's Perspective as a Radical Critique of Sociology." *Sociological Inquiry* 44, no. 1: 7–13.

Star, Susan Leigh. 2010. "This Is Not a Boundary Object: Reflections on the Origin of a Concept." *Science, Technology & Human Values* 35, no. 5: 601–17. https://doi.org/10.1177/0162243910377624.

Star, Susan Leigh, and J. R. Griesemer. 1989. "Institutional Ecology, 'Translations,' and Boundary Objects: Amateurs and Professionals in Berkeley's Museum of Vertebrate Zoology, 1907–39." *Social Studies of Science* 19, no. 3: 387–420. https://doi.org/10.1177/030631289019003001.

Stewart, Katherine. 2020. *The Power Worshipers: Inside the Dangerous Rise of Religious Nationalism.* New York: Bloomsbury Publishing.

Stewart, Kathleen. 2007. *Ordinary Affects.* Durham, N.C.: Duke University Press.

Venturini, T. 2021. "Toward a Sociology of Online Monsters: Online Conspiracy Theories and the Secondary Orality of Digital Platforms." https://hal.science/hal-03464174.

Viverios de Castro, E. 2004. "Exchanging Perspectives: The Transformation of Objects into Subjects in Amerindian Ontology." *Common Knowledge Symposium* 10, no. 3.

Wendling, Mike. 2018. *Alt-Right: From 4chan to the White House*. Winnipeg: Fernwood Publishing.

Williams, Daniel K. 2010. God's Own Party: The Making of the Christian Right. New York: Oxford University Press.

Williams, Michael, and Catherine Marfin. 2021. "Qanon Supporters Gather in downtown Dallas Expecting JFK Jr. to Reappear." *The Dallas Morning News.* Accessed April 26, 2023. https://www.dallasnews.com/news/2021/11/02/qanon-supporters-gather-in-downtown-dallas-expecting-jfk-jr-to-reappear/.

3

Galton Reloaded: Computer Vision and Machinic Eugenics

Giselle Beiguelman

As we all know, computers do not see. When we refer to computer vision, we point to a system that can read, interpret, and extract data from digital files. Its application encompasses OCR (optical character recognition), medical images, search engines, 3D modeling, surveillance, biometrics, self-driving cars, and various image editing techniques (Szeliski 2011, 3–8). Present in various activities, computer-vision systems operate as filters and lenses of our daily lives or as apparatus. In Michel Foucault's terms lately updated by Giorgio Agamben, the apparatus concerns "a heterogeneous set, linguistic and nonlinguistic, which includes virtually anything under the same title: discourses, institutions, buildings, laws, security measures, philosophical propositions," which results "from the crossings of relations of power and relations of knowledge" (Agamben 2009, 29; reverse translation by the author).

It is through this crossing of relations of power and relations of knowledge that computer vision is discussed in this essay. While "interpreting" the visible, computer-vision algorithmic models shape fields of visibility and invisibility, producing new forms of exclusion and control. Interpretation, in this case, does not involve any hermeneutic operations. In the same way that computers do not see, they also do not understand images at any level of representation. The image for the computer has no semiotic or aesthetical meaning. In computational terms, it is just a matrix of points and blocks that allow an A.I. to identify patterns such as edges, shapes, textures, curves, corners, and colors and group them through filters. This seems obvious, but the recurrence of metaphors around computer vision tends to blur this primary instance.

This kind of metaphor refers structurally to the anthropocentric paradigms of artificial intelligence. First, there is the basic assumption that to be intelligent is to be human and that intelligence must mirror human attributes like human vision or natural language processing (NLP), where language means human vernacular language, with American English as a default paradigm. Not less relevant is the supposition that intelligence is an exclusive attribute of the human brain, despite different multispecies approaches, such as those by Donna Haraway, Anna Tsing, Eduardo de Castro, and James Bridle, among many others. The association of deep-learning algorithms and neural networks departs from this set of assumptions, aiming to mimic the human brain, from a neurological point of view, through multiple layers of interconnected nodes.

This is the case of convolutional neural networks (CNNs), a type of machine learning commonly used in computer-vision tasks—designed to process data with a gridlike structure, such as an image. The process of training a CNN involves presenting it with a large dataset of examples and adjusting the weights of the connections between the nodes in the network so that it can learn to recognize patterns and features in the data. Once the CNN has been trained, it can be used to make predictions or classify new data based on its learned features. Nevertheless, vision is not just a physiological attribute mobilized by neurology; it is inseparable from the subjectivity forms shaped in different historical conditions and one of the layers of the body's social production, topics extensively reviewed by Jonathan Crary on more than one occasion (Crary 1991; 2000). Therefore, when referring to computer vision, computer sciences express the worldviews that modeled their approaches to technology.

It would be unfair to assume that computer scientists are unaware that human vision is relational, integrated with other senses and thoughts, and "does much more than just recognize objects." However, despite recognizing the immense differences between human vision and machine, they usually understand these differences as problems to be solved by improving the data-training process, a prerogative of machine learning (Goodfellow, Bengio, and Courville 2016, 366–67).

Machine learning involves the development of algorithms and statistical models that allow computers to learn and make decisions or predictions based on data without being explicitly programmed to perform a specific task. From a contemporary educational point of view, machine-learning principles would be considered a failure even considering the complexity of the operations involved in models for visual data, such as convolutional neural networks. They reproduce what educator Paulo Freire defined as a banking model of education (*educação bancária*). Based on operations of deposit, accumulation, and reproduction of knowledge, this pedagogical model is hierarchical and supposes the superiority of the professor and not partnerships between its agents. Because of this, according to Freire, it suppresses the emergence of alterity and narration, neutralizing critical points of view and creativity (Freire 2018, 79–83). The analysis of machine learning from a pedagogical perspective falls beyond the scope of this essay. However, it reinforces that artificial intelligence is not an abstract framework that plays out its rules in an autonomous parallel universe. It is a cultural construct firmly assented in historical dynamics of power, in which the anthropocentric reference, based on the white man's superiority, plays a central role.

The Society of Biased Data

Several studies show how biased data reinforce stereotypes and make Black individuals more vulnerable in surveillance systems (Buolamwini and Gebru 2018; Silva 2022). However, the "discipline and punish" relationship is only one of the many current racist biopolitical strategies of domination. In what concerns healthcare, a terrain where the role of A.I. is essential and increasing its prominence rapidly, biased datasets impact diagnosis predictions and priority in the access to services (Owens and Walker 2020, 1327). Of course, improving the quality of data that feeds the computer-vision models is possible. This may include different strategies of data review, like public information about the data collected (Zou and Schiebinger 2018, 325), and the development of technologies to depurate the biased information (Steed and Caliskan 2021).

Developing a computer-vision model demands vast amounts of data and a preliminary labeling process of thousands of images that will allocate data in different categories or classes and feed the machine-learning process. Nevertheless, algorithms do not execute their tasks spontaneously. Analyzing ImageNet, a dataset used by many computer-vision systems, Crawford and Paglen showed the genealogy of the prejudices they embed. For example, the "human body" category is in the Natural object > Body > Human body branch, and its subcategories are distributed between males and females according to their age profile (adult or juvenile). "As the 'adult body' includes the subclasses 'adult female' body and 'adult male body,' we find an implicit assumption here: only 'male' and 'female' bodies are 'natural'" (Crawford and Paglen 2019).

Labels, as we see, play a pivotal role in the social production of biased data-embedding prejudices in the hierarchies and in the identification of the images that will be used in machine-learning tasks. Workers hired for specific tasks on remote platforms such as Amazon Mechanical Turk (AMT) usually begin the labeling process. These workers constitute an emerging global precariat, performing decontextualized and atomized tasks in a global system of platformed labor. Underpaid and unprepared for image interpretation, they reveal what Marx defined as alienation in the labeling processes, the disconnection of labor from the worker experience (Moreschi et al. 2020; Grohmann et al. 2022).

Other important factors for understanding how data becomes biased are economical and geopolitical. For economic reasons, unsupervised systems are becoming more relevant, amplifying the problems of the social production of data. These use pretrained models through *transfer learning* to images not previously labeled, multiplying their identification mistakes and biases. Pretrained models feed facial analysis applications, which can be used in security systems but also in many other contexts. They can also be used in the hiring process with software that conducts video interviews, examines them, and sorts the job candidates based on machine decisions, combining natural language processing (NLP) and computer-vision models. One of the most recurrent complaints of users of this kind of service is about the obscure methodology of the sorting process and the role of biased data in the process (Harwell 2019; EPIC 2019).

Finally, another factor in the production chain of biased data is geopolitical. Concerning the computer-vision field, 45 percent of the 14 million labeled images from ImageNet come from the United States, a country that constitutes 4 percent of the global population. In contrast, China and India, which together represent 36 percent of the global population, account for a mere 3 percent of the images in the same database (Zou and Schiebinger 2018, 325). In short:

> Several commercial computer-vision systems (Microsoft, IBM, Face++) have been criticized due to their asymmetric accuracy across sub-demographics in recent studies. These studies found that the commercial face gender classification systems perform better on male and light faces. Various unwanted biases in image datasets occur due to biased selection, capture, and negative sets. Most

public large-scale face datasets have been collected from
popular online media—newspapers, Wikipedia, or web
search—and these platforms are more frequently used by
or showing White people. (Karkkainen and Joo 2021)

Algorithmic Racism

The profile and amount of data are essential to understanding
the architecture of algorithmic-based biases. Within the scope
of historical colonialism, a broad spectrum of scientific theories
supported racism, ranging from Linnaeus's classification of the
different profiles of *homo sapiens* to the phrenological, phisio-
nomical, ethnographic, and eugenicist studies. Those theories,
which hierarchized white men's superiority, played a crucial role in
naturalizing the routines of appropriation, subjugation, and extermination of Blacks and Indigenous peoples during the nineteenth
and twentieth centuries (Schwarcz 1999). Today, data colonialism
reinforces those excluding practices.

The notion of data colonialism assumes "the social relations
embodied in data are part of a broader colonial (and not merely
capitalist) legacy" (Couldry and Mejias 2019, 85). Performing
dynamics of power, those relations do not replace the traditional
forms of expropriation. However, they include data appropriation
and its transformation in corporate capital and social resources.
The nomination of the new James Bond to succeed Daniel Craig,
the protagonist for the fifth and last time in the famous spy film
series (*No Time to Die*, 2021), elucidate those data relations. It was
the first case of "assisted casting" by artificial intelligence, and the
chosen actor was Henry Cavill, famous for the role of Superman in
Batman vs. Superman—The Origin of Justice (2016) (LargoFilms 2020).

Like any prediction supported by data analysis, conclusions
depend on the amount of data and their quality. Even though it is
a nomination and not the definitive choice, the selection reveals
the dynamics of algorithmic racism. Furthermore, the data profile
that trained the algorithms explains why it was not a woman or a

Black actor or actress selected to replace Craig. To find the new James Bond, Largo Films developed a system fed with thousands of attributes of the character, from physical features to narrative elements, to identify his "DNA footprint." The development of the program results from a machine-learning process that computed analyses of metadata from more than 400,000 films, 1.8 million actors, and 59,000 scripts.

The numbers are gigantic ("robust," to use the jargon). However, it translates into data the American film industry profile, which includes the incipient participation of Blacks and other ethnic minorities among its protagonists. At the time of the historic #OscarSoWhite campaign in 2016, statistics showed that between 1928 and 2015, only 1 percent of nonwhite women and 6.8 percent of nonwhite men were Oscar winners. This number quadrupled in 2019, reaching 27.6 percent, which shows that even with this increase, the movie industry is far from reflecting race and gender social diversity (Bruce-Lockhart, Faunce, and Burn-Murdoch 2020).

Black protagonists are few and do not correspond to the metadata associated with James Bond's attributes. Therefore, the "so white" character of this cultural economy sector implies the impossibility for Largo Films' A.I. to match the expectations of nominating a Black woman or man for the role of James Bond. Datasets compiled for the selection are poor in these references reflecting the presence of structural racism in society and expanding it in new directions. After all, when looking for a new Bond based on what has always been the old Bond, one could hardly expect a result very different from confirmation of the same James Bond pattern. A white man with a beautiful woman with decorative functions.

This is not "natural" of the algorithm itself (a set of mathematical rules that inform an action) but of its modeling. Some of its harmful consequences include targeted search results, such as hypersexualized images for "black girls" and automatically tagging Black people as gorillas on Google. Another example is selfie "beautification" apps through the whitening of pictures, as shown by studies by

Safiya Noble, author of *Algorithms of Oppression* (2018). In the same direction, research conducted by two Brazilian scholars, Tarcizio Silva and André Mintz, analyzed the performance of pretrained computer-vision models from Google, IBM, and Microsoft, investigating their interpretations of 16,000 images related to Brazilians, Nigerians, Austrians, and Portuguese. One of the questions of the study was to understand how these computer-vision systems label phenotypic characteristics of nonwhite people and non-Western symbols, emphasizing Indigenous and Black peoples. The study revealed, for example, that Google Cloud Vision assigns the tag "wig" to black women with curly hair or turbans, explicating its cultural limits (Silva et al. 2020).

It is not by chance that so many errors in the identification of Black people occur with face-recognition systems; this was the argument of the documentary *Coded Bias* (2020). Shalini Kantayya's film premiered at the Sundance Film Festival and focused on the artist Joy Buolamwini, at the time a student at Massachusetts Institute of Technology (MIT). For an art project at MIT, Buolamwini tried to develop a mirror that would put other faces over hers. Nevertheless, the facial-recognition software could not detect her face until she decided to put on a white mask. It was the beginning of an activist investigation into how algorithms mainly affect Black women. Although the documentary focuses on the political dimensions of computer vision in our daily lives, those technologies are far from impacting only the quotidian. They also affect the perception of the past and the politics of memory, contributing to historical denialism via different sorts of deepfakes.

Deepfakes Trues

The term *deepfake* is a neologism that appeared in November 2017 on Reddit. It was initially the user's nickname and the forum's name dedicated to applying deep-learning technologies to swap the faces of porn actresses for celebrity faces (Cole 2018). Reddit banned the group one year later, but the spread of A.I. technologies on the Internet consolidated the deepfake routines available in different apps and social media, allowing anyone to be a pop star or a politi- cian for a few seconds.

It is a commonplace to say that after Photoshop nobody is surprised by image manipulations anymore and that image appropriation of politicians is not new. Stalinism extensively used adulterated photos, and Nazism and fascism defrauded countless others. Nevertheless, it is worth emphasizing that deepfake is neither collage nor editing and dubbing. A deepfake is an algorithmic image without human mediation in its processing. It uses thousands of stored photos in datasets to learn a person's facial movements, including lip-synching and voice modulations, to predict and depict how that person would say something they never said. One of the technologies used for creating deepfakes is the StyleGANs (Generative Adversarial Networks for Style-Based Generation of Faces), a neural-network architecture specifically for face generation. Unlike the CNNs process, which is oriented to classify and predict behaviors, StyleGANs images are trained to incorporate aesthetic attributes, such as lighting, curves, and contrasts. They also distribute a face's elements from other images, adopting its characteristics and looking more convincing (Karras et al. 2020; Altuncu, Franqueira, and Li 2022).

One of the most well-known uses of this technology is the *This Person Does Not Exist* project. The pictures on the project website are initially intriguing and vivid, making one believe that the portraits it hosts are of real people. However, they are also intriguing because they prescind the gaze, as algorithms trained by machine-learning systems synthesize (generate) them. Thus, they write a new chapter in the history of postphotography, which had already discarded the need for a camera, a topic addressed by several thinkers, such as Joanna Zylinska (2017), and photographers, such as Joan Fontcuberta (2007). However, beyond the discussions about the veracity, appropriation, and clashes between humans and machines, an eternal issue of technical image, we should consider deepfakes in the political realm of alt-right and creationist movements, as shown in the artwork *In Event of Moon Disaster* (Panetta and Burgund 2020).

In this video installation, President Richard Nixon reports, directly from the White House Oval Office, the Apollo 11 disaster. His speech was written by William Safire and would be read in the event of an accident with the 1969 Lunar Mission. For that, an MIT team used Richard Nixon's filmed speeches to transfer his facial expressions and lip movements to his clone, with his voice, diction, and facial expressions, saying words he never said about an event that never occurred. The artwork draws attention to the potential damage of deepfakes in terms of historical revisionism, a particularly relevant topic nowadays, given the increasing manipulation of the past by different denialist far-right movements.

No less relevant are the recurrent historical appropriations for commercial purposes, which have been transforming cultural memory into a commodity. Concerning this, art critic T. J. Clark wrote that, if previously capitalism used to sell promises of the future, today it produces objects "to invent a story, a lost time of intimacy and stability, which everyone claims to remember, but no one ever had." Clark identified the need to fictionalize the past with a time crisis, marked by the "attempt to expel the banality of the present from consciousness" (Clark 2007, 322–23; reverse translation by the author).

Before him, Umberto Eco showed that this type of movement also paved the way for "a philosophy of immortality as duplication." As if we could not experience the past anymore, it was only possible to reproduce it, not preserve it through memory. This approach fosters a thematic approach to institutions and social spaces that consolidate the past's permanent setting as architecture or an image (Eco 1984, 12–19). The scenographic approach to the past tends to transform the lived moment into a monument to the present that was not. On the one hand, we could say we live in a state of documental overdose, compulsively recording our daily lives with the camera phone, which became a kind of third eye in the palm of the hand, continually scanning life. On the other, we submerge in the impossibility of accessing memory, following

the timeline logic of social media, ordered according to the more
recent event.

Instead of contributing to new archival models, the documental
overdose pasteurizes history through trivializing images, as
shown in *Yolocaust.* In this work, Shapira (2017) explored "our
commemorative culture by combining selfies from the Holocaust
Memorial in Berlin with footage from Nazi extermination camps,"
the artist explains on the project website. The pictures came from
social media and dating apps, and all received new captions, like
"Jumping on dead Jews @ Holocaust Memorial," but keeping their
original "Likes."

The same phenomenon of neutralizing traumatic experience via
social media surrounded *Barca Nostra* (2019) but for different
reasons. An artwork by Swiss-Icelandic artist Christoph Büchel, who
rebuilt the fishing boat that sank in the Mediterranean in 2015, kill-
ing 800 people, it was presented at the 58th Venice Biennale. In few
days, it became an Instagram cliché, despite the artist's intention
to focus on the greatest tragedy of the current migration crisis. The
insertion of the same Barca Nostra and its tragic memories in an
appealing scenario, such as the city of Venice, transformed the idea
of mobilizing the political awareness of the Biennale visitors into a
"beautiful" background for smiling faces and banal images.

The forms of image production and circulation today say a lot about
memory status in digital time. There is a compulsion for archiving
today. Everything is registered in the eagerness to "save" a moment,
and one cannot ignore how "saving" memories are symptomatic of
digital-culture ambivalences toward archiving. Everything must be
recorded, captured, and posted, even if it is to be erased in twenty-
four hours. However, this archiving fever parallels the pop culture
of remakes. As music critic Simon Reynolds says, we live in an age
where everything is "re" (remakes, re-records, reprints, revivals)
and is entirely for sale through the "new" add-on. "Instead of being
about itself, the 2000s have been about every other previous
decade happening again all at once" (Reynolds 2012).

Botox Memory

There are Formica kitchen designs, mini-scooters, cars inspired by famous 1930s models, rockabilly hairstyles, and hippie and punk clothes for all. Retro design is everywhere, and the "user experience" (UX) legitimizes the demand for memory as a consumer good. Anthropologist Arjun Appadurai calls this phenomenon "imagined nostalgia," a result of merchandising techniques, which creates experiences of losses that never happened (Appadurai 1996, 76–77). It is possible to locate this movement in the 1990s when the frontiers of the debate on collective memory transcended academic boundaries and gained contours of transnational and media events. Some remarkable moments of this process were the celebration of the fiftieth anniversary of World War II, the one-year celebrations of the fall of the Berlin Wall, and the ten years since the end of Latin American dictatorships. Newspaper supplements covering all those events, TV specials, commissions for new architectural landmarks, public artworks, and a large production of books and films are all icons of that "memory boom" of the 1990s (Huyssen 2009, 15; 2014, 39).

Nevertheless, thirty years after the boom of memory as a commodity so typical of the 1990s, we face a different situation. The Anthropocene erodes old prospects for the future and what prevails is the uberization of life, constricted by the norms of techno-financial automatism. The proliferation of cell phone apps to three-dimensionalize, colorize, and animate old photos, giving "life" to the past, indicates that we have expanded the idea of memory as a commodity to one of history as a gadget. An emblematic case of this search for a mythic past was the launch of Deep Nostalgia in 2021. A powerful combination of "gadgetization" of history with deepfake technologies, Deep Nostalgia allowed animation of old photos, from personal ancestors to historical personalities, giving them expressions through smiles and blinking eyes and movement with head turns, amusing millions.

The Deep Nostalgia algorithm is built with several deep neural networks trained with datasets of thousands of videos. It searches prerecorded videos from the database and calculates its movements to interpolate its pixels onto the static photo. An occlusion map synthesizes the missing parts in the picture and adds them to the system, revealing teeth, the side of the head, and other aspects absent in the original image. This computational odyssey produces, in seconds, the natural look of the animations. The success of computer-vision models like those used by Deep Nostalgia is symptomatic not only of the potential of A.I.s for creating "deep faked pasts" but of the ambivalences of our relationship to the experience of history.

The proliferation of applications for aging one's face thirty years, or those that remove wrinkles, is a sign that we have abolished the "past as past" (Pelbart 2007, 70) or at least the past as we knew it. In tune with this approach, 3D models of "revitalization" projects designed for historical areas present urban sites processed, as it were, with Botox injections applied to city landscapes. They incorporate the anti-aging techniques of human bodies in the urban realm, "giving tourists the impression that they are in the eternity of a postcard" (Jeudy and Berenstein 2006, 9).

On the one hand, "tomorrow is now," as we learned from the Museu do Amanhã (Museum of Tomorrow) slogan at the time of its construction in Rio de Janeiro. On the other hand, given the increasingly recurrent ecological catastrophes, climate changes caused by human action, and the exponential increase in technological waste produced daily, we may not have something to conserve. In this sense, "what would be driving conservation for the future is no longer the anguish of the loss of traces, but the fear of not having anything to transmit" (Jeudy 2005, 46; reverse translation by the author).

The Privatization of the Gaze

It goes beyond the limits of this essay to discuss the role of technology companies in environmental degradation. However, one cannot ignore that the same corporations monopolizing numerous sectors of contemporary social life are behind the software and hardware of all those systems. Google, Meta, and Amazon cross the most diverse social life activities. StyleGAN was developed in the laboratories of Nvidia, a leading company in graphics processing units (GPUs) and the artificial intelligence market. Microsoft, the owner of the cloud computing service Azure, is one of the main investors of OpenAi, responsible for the new revolution in using NLP techniques in creative activities.

The contemporary politics of the image refers to the possibility of corporate control of the gaze on an unprecedented scale. Even though partnerships do not necessarily imply affiliations and these agreements go back to the history of photography, no photographic company had a monopoly on some of our basic infrastructures (Goldenfein 2020). The pioneer *Logo.Hallucination* (2006), by artist Christophe Bruno, anticipates some possible political and cultural developments from the corporate control of computer-vision technologies, infrastructures, and products. For its realization, Bruno used image-recognition technologies "in order to detect subliminal forms of logos or emblems, hidden (involuntarily) in the visual environment or in the whole of Internet images" (Bruno 2006). As a result, a Vermeer painting would already contain the Atari games logo; an African mask would be the original McDonald's; a bikini would be the original shape of the Mercedes-Benz brand, among other bizarre cases documented on the project's website.

Bruno showed how the new features of pattern recognition in images became a fertile field for copyright management, as they could reach such a degree of hallucination that would culminate in the privatization of the gaze. This is made explicit in the ways social media platforms block supposed immoral content according to their rules. Images portraying nudity are usually understood as sexually suggestive, no matter if they are historical materials, contemporary art, or an affective moment of a mother breastfeeding her child. Interpreted as sensitive content, they tend to be automatically removed from the users' profiles. How giants like Instagram make these identifications is unclear to their users. It is not the point here to try to discover how Instagram algorithms work (one of the most hidden secrets of the digital industry) but to stress how their monitoring practices enunciate a new kind of censorship, one that does not forbid it. Instead, it defines algorithmically the right of what can be seen and how. This dynamic essentially refers to the role of patterns in today's visual vocabulary.

> Most of the contemporary applications of machine learn-
> ing can be described according to the two modalities of
> classification and prediction, which outline the contours
> of a new society of control and statistical governance.
> Classification is known as pattern recognition, while pre-
> diction can also be defined as pattern generation. A new
> pattern is recognized or generated by interrogating the
> inner core of the statistical model. (Pasquinelli and Joler
> 2020, 13)

It is no coincidence that all the deepfake images in *This Person Does Not Exist* have the same look and a poker-face smile. Built with images scraped from the Internet, they mirror how people present themselves online, usually as heroes of their own lives. Neverthe-less, deepfakes illuminate other intricacies of the standardization of visuality. These intricacies refer to the production chain involving cameras, less dependent on lenses and sensors and more on arti-ficial intelligence, to image-processing programs and the channels through which they flow (mainly social media).

Together they respond to and model the standardized format-ting of perspectives, colors, and points of view that multiply on networks and spread in common cellphone camera resources like auto-alignment. Some people will undoubtedly say that countless times the pattern does not correspond to what was intended to be registered, and it is possible to revert it. However, given the path of the digital market, we can say the forthcoming cameras, increas-ingly "smart," will learn to capture "corrected" photos, making it difficult to disobey their prefabricated designs.

This denotes the presence of computer vision in our daily lives and how we naturalize its rules in cultural expression. We live in the paradoxical situation of potentially creating the wealthiest and most plural visual culture in history through access to media and diving into the limbo of gaze uniformity. However, uniformity here is intrinsically related to predictability. So, artificial intelligence puts us in front of a new machine/eye operation, an inseparable binomial in contemporary times, as shown by the work of artist Harun Farocki (1944–2014).

With the increasing amount of data and more efficient mathematical models in development, machines can achieve higher accuracy levels in terms of capacity to preview the results. This predictability profoundly affects our ways of seeing, perceiving, and figuring out reality. It is enough here to recall the selfie phenomenon to corroborate this statement. After all, it has permanently changed the self-portrait's angle, which is no longer frontal, corresponding to the camera on the tripod. It has adapted to the available angle for capturing with a cell phone, from 7 to 17 degrees, as seen in the *Selfiecity* project (Manovich 2014).

The selfie standard cannot be dissociated from the algorithmic rules that conditionate visibility in social media and project it to the social realm. The liberal economy of "Likes," and its successful formulas, tends to homogenize everything we produce and see. It standardizes angles, frames, scenes, and styles. What is behind this are the criteria for organizing the data so that it is more quickly "findable" in online searches and how the algorithms contextualize the contents in the specific bubbles to which we belong (something that we do not control but that controls us). In this sense, paraphrasing Foucault in *Discipline and Punish,* algorithms are the disciplinary apparatus of our time, which gains efficiency as people try to respond to their rules to become visible. From this perspective, it is possible to understand how the platformed society operates as a social Darwinist device of exclusion that may be pointing to new forms of eugenics: machinic eugenics of the gaze.

Eugenics is a word derived from the Greek *eugenes,* and it means "well-born, good stock, and noble race." British scientist Francis Galton (1822–1911) coined the term *eugenics* in 1883 in the book *Inquiries into Human Faculty and Its Development.* His motivation was to offset the "slowness" of the processes of natural selection that Darwin, his cousin, theorized about, granting, in *The Descent of Man*, that, "At some future period, not very distant as measured by centuries, the civilized races of man will almost certainly extermi-nate and replace throughout the world the savage races" (Darwin 1896, 156). Nevertheless, for Galton this was too much time, and he dedicated himself to creating technologies to improve the human species. Looking to change the composition of populations and favoring the reproduction of certain types to the detriment of others, Galton dedicated himself to adapting the ideas of artificial selection Darwin explained in the first pages of *On the Origin of Species,* studying the selective breeding practiced by farmers.

Proposed as a science, eugenics soon became a social and inter-national movement. In 1907 the Eugenics Education Society was founded in Great Britain. The same year marked the approval of the first laws on sterilizing Blacks and the prohibition of interracial marriages in the United States. There, the American Eugenics Record Office existed with this name until the end of the 1960s. In 1913, dermatologist and psychiatrist Iwan Blocht founded the Medical Society for Sexology and Eugenics in Germany. Another country on the vanguard in this field was Brazil, whose Eugenics Society dates to the 1920s. The new science spread worldwide within a few years, followed by laws and governmental acts target-ing Indigenous and Black populations. In Nazi Germany, eugenics became the official policy of the state starting in 1933, with the aim of exterminating mainly the Jewish people but also other groups considered "undesirable" by the Nazi regime. This delirium resulted in the alarming number of deaths: 6 million Jews, 250,000 Sinti, at least 200,000 mentally ill, an unknown number of Black people, and many thousands of homosexuals, communists, and political opponents, classified as 'antisocial' (Beiguelman 1997; Eugenics Archive, 2015).

For the development of his theories about eugenics, Galton created composite portraiture, a photographic method superimposing several faces from multiple exposures onto the same plate. He erased all individualized features from the result to get a generic face identifying a specific biological and social profile. As Galton said, the aim was to reach "with mechanical precision" a "generalized picture [. . .] that represents no man in particular but portrays an imaginary figure possessing the average features of any given group of men" (Galton 1879, 132–33). He inferred this supposed precision from interpreting his methodology as "pictorial statistics" (Galton 1883, 233).

Galton's composite portraits thus indicate the belief, as Allan Sekula (1986) says, in the confluence of methods resulting from statistics with optics. This belief is not exclusive to Galton and brings him closer to another famous character in the history of photography, Alphonse Bertillon (1853–1914), and his criminological image. Both scientists shared the belief in the existence of the "average man" (*L'homme moyen*), a concept by one of the pioneers of statistical science, the Belgian Adolphe Quételet (1796–1874). This quantitative method legitimizes, for Galton and Bertillon, the passage from the purely optical to the purely datafied, or from the empirical to the irrefutable scientific proof of the criminal biotype (Sekula 1986, 18–22; Lee-Morrison 2019, 95).

In *The Normalizing Machine* (2018), an interactive installation by Mushon Zer-Aviv, each participant is presented with four previously recorded videos of other participants and should point at the "most normal" among them. Algorithms examine the selected person and add their image to a database projected on a wall reproducing Bertillon's anthropometric boards. It is surprising to see, in seconds, one's image scanned into measurements of eyes, mouth, and ears and computed with hundreds of other participants. However,

the face treated as a computational model (Kember 2014, 186)
determines new models of standardization of bodies following the
A.I.'s assumptions.

Zer-Aviv defines his project as an experiment in machine learning
and algorithmic prejudice. He recalls, however, that the founding
father of computing and artificial intelligence, the English math-
ematician Alan Turing (1912–1954), "hoped A.I. would transcend
the kind of systemic bias that criminalized his deviation from
the norms" (Zer-Aviv 2018). In his now classic article "Computing Machinery and Intelligence" (1950), Turing proposed that
computer-based machine learning should be based on the child's
brain and not the adult's (Turing 1950, 456).

Not by chance did Turing discuss learning machines and not
machine learning, meaning machines that can learn instead of the
machinic process of learning. The challenge, he said, would be to
design computers with unlimited storage, capable of dealing with
random programming, assuming that "the rules which get changed
in the learning process are of a rather less pretentious kind, claim-
ing only an ephemeral validity" (Turing 1950, 458). The contextual
mutability of rules breaks the hierarchical-learning model based
on errors and successes. Moreover, its random performance
confronts the aimed homogeneity of highly repressive societies,
intolerant of otherness, such as the one in which Turing himself, as
a gay man, lived. In some ways, as Zer-Aviv speculates, his thought
expressed a reaction to a social model and an attempt to respond
to the oppression of his person through a mathematical notation.

In its beginnings, we can also say that artificial intelligence was
much closer to technodiversity and the recursive model of which
Chinese philosopher Yuk Hui (2020) speaks than to the normalizing
model that Zer-Aviv's work criticizes. *The Normalizing Machine*
discusses what and how society sets as the standard for normality
and how A.I. and machine-learning processes can amplify the
discriminatory tendencies that ancient anthropometric theories
underpinned centuries ago.

The links between the history of photography and biopolitical control have been widely discussed and directly or indirectly refer to Michel Foucault's seminal analysis of the panopticon (Foucault 1995, 195–228). In the colonialist realm, photography played an essential role in legitimizing scientific racist discourse, intertwining studies of visual representation with sciences, as shown by different scholars (Machado and Huber 2010; Fischer 2019; Azoulay 2019, 36). However, no discriminatory scientific discourse had the influence and longevity of the ideas and methodologies created by Galton, which had impacts from face recognition to the eugenics revival in biotechnologies.

From Pictorial Statistics to Statistical Photography

Face recognition is an application of computer vision that involves machine-learning algorithms and statistical analysis to examine and identify faces in images and video. The system requires the ability to detect and analyze facial features, such as the shape of the face, the distance between the eyes, and the structure of the cheekbones, as Bertillon did. With those elements, a facial recognition system creates a unique numerical signature or "template" for each face, compares this template to a database of known faces, and determines the person's identity in the image.

In a tentative genealogy of the machinic gaze, face recognition marks an aesthetic and political encounter of computer vision with the nineteenth-century imagination. It is noteworthy how the numerical signature used in face recognition systems resembles Quételet's "average man" concept in that it is a statistical summary of specific characteristics of a face. Quételet used this concept to describe the standard of a population's features, such as height and weight, which could describe the "typical" individual in that population (Grue and Heiberg 2006). However, the template used in facial recognition systems is specifically designed to identify individual faces rather than to describe the average characteristics of a population, as Galton's, expanding Quételet's, ideas did.

Despite all the terrible consequences eugenics had in the Second World War, some researchers recovered this background, acclaiming face recognition's promises to identify criminal biotypes. Like the father of criminal anthropology, Cesare Lombroso (1835–1909), an early adopter of the composite portraits, these studies assume that it is possible to identify the profile of the criminal individual through the analysis of facial characteristics and the emotions they express. In a controversial article published in 2016, two investigators from Shanghai Jiao Tong University announced a computer-vision model for inference on criminality using face images. Based on the analysis of 1,856 photos, the authors say, "the most important discovery of this research is that criminal and non-criminal face images populate two quite distinctive manifolds" (Wu and Zhang 2016). The publication includes illustrative scientific images of the most common biotypes of criminals and noncriminals in the best Galtonian style. Contested by many and still a reference for others, its approach is far from being an exception, as we can see in an article published in 2020 in the *Journal of Big Data*, one of the top-rank of journals in its field (Hashemi and Hall 2020).

Another polemic article must be cited here. Published in the *Journal of Personality and Social Psychology* in 2018 and written by two Stanford University investigators by this time, it sought to demonstrate, based on 30,000 images extracted from a dating site, that computer vision could reveal, from facial analysis, who were the gay people, with 81 percent accuracy (Wang and Kosinski 2018). "Essentially, it [the article] suggested that computers could have better 'gaydar' than gay humans themselves, with an accuracy rate 'comparable with mammograms or modern diagnostic tools for Parkinson's disease'" (Belden-Adams 2020, 215).

These scientific texts share the belief that face recognition results are neutral and trustworthy because they are based on algorithms and statistics. Galton called his composite portraits "pictorial statistics" not for the rhetorical effect of the definition but because he is the founding father of regressive statistics, a paradigm of any machine-learning process and pivotal for understanding the relations of pattern recognition and eugenics. From Galton's point of view, his composite technique that looked for coincident patterns, erasing individual traces, would contribute to the "betterment" of the British population. Given the abstraction of those methodologies, it is difficult here not to agree with researcher Daniel Novak when he says that Galton created a scheme that "would make photographic fiction into photographic science—a non-existent body into a type derived with scientific accuracy, a photographic science fiction" (Novak 2004, 58). However, as consistent as Novak's statement may sound, some computer-vision experiments show an ongoing revival of the British scientist's ideas and methodologies with significant social and political implications.

Eugenics Never Ended

By the end of the 1990s, the activist collective Critical Art Ensemble pointed out that some biotechnological findings refer to the conceptual and political realm of a "second wave of eugenics" due to its "promise to rationalize the gene pool in a way that seems economically and socially productive to capitalist forces" (Critical Art Ensemble 1998, 127). Their prognostics can be confirmed in basic searches in scientific databases for uses of Genetic Algorithms, which express positive ideas toward their machinic eugenics powers.

Genetic algorithm is a term that refers to the use of artificial intelligence to enhance or alter the genetic makeup of living organisms. This involves using A.I. to analyze an organism's DNA, identifying specific genetic variations that could be targeted for modification or enhancement. It may also include using A.I. to design and synthesize new genetic material. These technologies could improve the health and well-being of humans and other living organisms by eliminating inherited diseases and disabilities or enhancing certain traits that benefit the individual or society. All those possibilities involve ethical decisions, and because of this, many scientists expressed concerns about the potential ethical and social implications of such technologies.

One can remember the reactions to the announcement of the first designer babies by Chinese scientist He Jiankui in 2014 (which later proved to be a fraud). This case was debated in the scientific community and widely reported in the media, showing that "molecular scissors" is far from consensual. It also showed that biotechnologies demand ethical and political debates beyond the possibility of creating a "genetic divide" between those who have access to these technologies and those who do not. They refer to human rights discussions and the prospect for abuse or misuse of these technologies by governments or other groups (Heritable Human Genome Editing 2020).

At the height of the Human Genome Project, a series of works were published addressing the expectations of human improvement, designer children, and a brighter future, free of diseases and sick people. Some of these works became bestsellers, such as that of Gregory Stock's *Redesigning Humans: Our Inevitable Genetic Future* (2002), published at the time he was the director of the Program on Medicine, Technology and Society at UCLA's School of Medicine. The book defends gene selection for the improvement of future generations and designer children, among others. Because of those positions, it is considered by many a defense of eugenics (Shaw n.d.).

Numerous statements by the geneticist James Watson, codiscoverer of the structure of DNA and a Nobel Prize laureate, in defense of "traditional" eugenics, are well known and aroused all sorts of protest. Watson had been the director of Cold Spring Harbor Laboratory since 1968, where the American Eugenics Record Office was founded in 1912. Given his known positions in favor of eugenics, his nomination as the director of the Human Genome Project (1988–1992) aroused concerns, linking biotechnological achievement with the eugenics past (Wilson 2017, 33–34). In the field of the humanities, the work of the philosopher of transhumanism, Nick Bostrom, openly argues in favor of a "new eugenics," aimed not at genocide but at the longevity and intelligence of posthumanity (Bostrom, Harris, and Savulescu 2018).

The Human Genome Project (HGP), the most significant scientific collaborative project in history, is not potentially eugenic. However, the myth of perfection many of its followers believe in is eugenic, not expressing scientifically what the genome is. As Armand Marie Leroi states:

> The human genome, the one whose sequence was published in *Nature* on 15 February 2001, is not a standard; it is merely a composite of the genomes of an unknown number of unknown people. As such, it has no special claim to normality or perfection (nor did the scientists who promoted and executed this great enterprise ever claim as much for it). This arbitrariness does not diminish in the slightest degree the value of this genomic sequence; after all, the genomes of any two people are 99.9 percent identical, so anyone's sequence reveals almost everything about everyone's. (Leroi 2005, 15)

Several factors could contribute to the development of machinic eugenics in the future, but no one is so relevant as the changes in societal attitudes. Nevertheless, in a biopolitical approach, positions, as summed up above, reveal an epistemology of the pattern reinforced by the role of A.I. technologies in defining new modalities of production of the normal, the average, and the standard, which point toward an age of machinic eugenics.

As discussed in the previous sections of this essay, A.I. technologies, particularly computer-vision models, amplify biases present in the data they are trained on, making decisions that reflect that bias, affecting our ways of seeing and perceiving the world. It is unlikely that A.I. will be able to control our gaze in the sense of physically forcing us to look at something. Still, A.I.-based computer-vision techniques can influence what we see and pay attention to, and can shape visuality. If machinic eugenics refers to the use of technology or machines to implement or facilitate eugenic practices or policies, machinic eugenics of the gaze refers to the ways of seeing following the standards established by the A.I.s.

Fictions of beauty play a crucial role in this process, mediating social interplays in popular platforms like Instagram and Tik Tok. It is commonplace to associate their algorithms with marketing profile analysis, but they are not less relevant concerning their users' subjectivities. The exponential growth of beautification apps contributes to idealizing specific standards that are difficult, not to say impossible, for most people to attain. Offered (actually sold) as filters and editing tools that allow users to alter their appearance, they function as pressuring devices to conform to certain beauty ideals, promoted and marketed on the same social media platforms.

Popular apps like Facetune, AirBrush, Perfect365, and YouCam Makeup, have among their primary tools filters to lighten skin tones, reinforce traditional gender roles like long eyelashes for women or a strong jawline for men, and for smoothing out wrinkles. Besides provoking feelings of inadequacy or low self-esteem, especially among young people (Chaderjian 2022; Rowland 2022), those beautification apps embody eugenicist assumptions that deserve some consideration in the scope of this essay. They rely mainly on the association of beauty with perfection and youth based on racial, gender-oriented, and ageist prejudices.

The correlation between racist standardized beauty ideals with youth is remarkable, given the role it played in the Aryan mythology of Nazism. Indeed, that kind of "cosmetic gaze" does not express itself in the politics of racial cleansing of the past and is not a result of, or specific to, social media. However, it stresses a constant repacking of oppressive cultural standards that used to target women (Wegenstein 2012, 151) but today encompasses many other social actors, adding new layers to the discussion of the eugenic imagination of our time.

The assertion about the eclipse of eugenics after the Second World War is recurrent, but it is not valid. Eugenics never ended. The discovery of structure of DNA by Francis Crick, with James Watson, in 1953, for which he received the Nobel Prize, "'emboldened' geneticists with eugenic sympathies. Crick was among the vanguard of this new interest in eugenics. In 1961, he called for a large-scale eugenics program" (Grue and Heiberg 2006, 243). Crick was far from being a lone voice. As can be seen in the book *Man and His Future* (1963), the chapter "Eugenics and Genetics" brings together several scientists, besides Crick, who argued for the reasonability of trying to improve the human species with eugenics techniques (Wolstenholme and Ciba Foundation 1963, 274–98).

Yet, the vitality of eugenics transcended the scientific debate. In the Nordic countries (Denmark, Finland, Iceland, Norway, and Sweden), eugenic sterilization laws were abolished only in the 1970s. In Sweden, they lasted until 1976, and in Norway until 1977. Applied for four decades, they resulted in more than 170,000 involuntary sterilizations (Nordstrom 2019). In Alberta and British Columbia (Canada), these laws were valid until the 1970s. The focus there was mostly on Indigenous women (Stone 2019). In India, forced sterilization laws were in effect from 1970 to 1977. However, they continued until the first decade of the 2000s, 4.6 million women were victims. In Australia, a country with a long history of eugenics, the separation of children from interracial marriages was systematic until the 1970s. Finally, in the United States, eugenics laws were in force from 1907 to 1970, resulting in 60,000 sterilizations, 20,000 of which were in California, particularly affecting Black women ("The Eugenics Archives" 2015).

From the 1970s onward, there was a shift from genetic studies to other disciplines such as psychology and social sciences, focusing on hereditary motivations for phenomena such as mental illness and criminality, as Tory Duster remarks:

> A review of the *Readers Guide to Periodical Literature* from 1976 to 1982 revealed a 231 percent increase in articles that attempted to explain the genetic basis for crime, mental illness, intelligence, and alcoholism during this brief six-year period. Even more remarkably, between 1983 and 1988, articles that attributed a genetic basis to crime appeared *more than four times* as frequently as they

had during the previous decade. This development in the popular print media was based in part upon what was occurring in the scientific journals. During this period, a new surge of articles (more than double the previous decade) appeared in the scientific literature, making claims about the genetic basis of several forms of social deviance and mental illness. (Duster 2003, 92)

These studies gained powerful impetus in the 1980s, and Duster (2003, 95–96) highlights the investments made by Ronald Reagan, then governor of California, in research related to the "genetics of criminals." The significant mediatic impact of those assumptions also intensified contrary positions, associating the eugenics past with emerging biotechnologies. In the context of the launch of the genome project, the defense of the improvement of specific traits replaced population improvement associated with racial extermination policies. Philosopher Robert A. Wilson calls those claims "newgenics" (2017, 86), given that, for historians, social scientists, and geneticists who defend its updating, the only problem with eugenics is the ghosts of mass extermination, not the reinforcement of the normal paradigm (Wilson 2017, 415).

The wide dissemination of artificial intelligence technologies has updated the controversial concept of normality in the mythology of the pattern, a prerogative, as discussed throughout this essay, of any process involving machine learning. Such normality is an abstract concept that refers to the sum of generic characteristics of a specific population group. It refers directly to the studies already mentioned here by Quételet and his conceptualization of the average man. This moral and physical construct became the rule (the norm) for eugenicists (Grue and Heiberg 2006, 234).

The biopolitical aspect of this notion of normal/pattern attribute allows consideration of the possibility of machinic eugenics of the gaze. As conceptualized by Foucault, modern biopolitics targeted the control of the workforce in the horizon of the demands of the industrial economy and the birth of modern urbanism. However, in the contemporary realm of the digital economy, biopolitics is a technology of power and control of the informational territories and its forms of occupation (Virilio 2012). Because of this, the biopolitics of the digital can target molecularly the bodies, going from the emotional sphere, based on individual performance in social networks, to physiological control. It is a kind of biopolitics that mobilizes technologies that penetrate bodies without touching them, a dynamic that Covid-19 made explicit through the proliferation of computer-vision tools, such as thermal cameras, to scan bodies all over the world continually. Nobody questions the need to use those technologies in a global sanitary crisis such as the coronavirus pandemic. Yet the opacity of its possible future uses shows that one of the big questions today is not *if* data is collected but by whom and for what purpose.

Computer-vision automation is far from being fair and neutral. It embeds prejudices of race, gender, and nationality and expresses ideological approaches to history. Because of this, it is an apparatus and not just a tool. Its increasing presence in almost all sectors and activities of our daily lives may transform it into the hegemonic visual apparatus of our time. This shift could be announcing an age of machinic eugenics of the gaze based on artificial intelligence regimes of vision. The hypothesis is plausible, given that Western vision regimes still refer to some rules of frames and windows inherited from the Renaissance. Although several technological experiences since the 2000s point to flexible displays and screenless projection systems, we are still attached to the classical canon of the rectangular format for our screens and reading devices (Friedberg 2009).

It is not a matter of adhering to a linear history of vision and the gaze that would assume the perspective device as the foundation of the hegemonic vision model since the Italian Quattrocento. Instead, this essay assumes that when we talk about vision, we are talking about ways of seeing, which imply their forms of social fabrication. If vision is a biological attribution and visuality a social fact (Foster 1998, ix), the gaze is the interplay of both. Nevertheless, this interplay considers the politics of aesthetics, "which defines what is visible or not in common space," and who can have or not a share in that space (Rancière 2004, 12–13).

The gaze, in this sense, goes beyond the field of vision. As we rely more on A.I. systems to process and interpret visual information, they may shape our perception and interpretation of the world to the way these systems see and understand it. The potential of artificial intelligence to shape fields of visibility will not imply genocide or racial wars, as the eugenic movements of the first half of the twentieth century did. Following computer-vision models, the machinic eugenics of the gaze may establish new forms of invisibility and social exclusion, thereby determining "the ability or inability to take charge of what is common to the community" and defining "what is visible or not in a common space" (Rancière 2004, 12–13).

The alternatives to improve computer-vision models via data cura-tion and improvement in machine-learning processes may solve punctual problems, but not the pattern-based model of current A.I. systems, and therefore not its dynamics of power and forms of the distribution of the sensible. New questions, and not answers, will come from counterhegemonic frameworks and not models. Those counterhegemonic models refer to feminist and queer studies, Standpoint and postnormal theories approach, and different educational systems, toward a "post–machine learning" culture and practice, as stated by Dan McQuillan (2022, 104–18). However, beyond this, reframing the A.I. standards will be possible only by considering backgrounds beyond the anthropocentric realms.

We may find different histories of algorithmic antagonism in mar-ginal forms of knowledge based on everyday practices, and their strategies for tactical ruptures, (Pereira et al. 2022, 125). As in the famous map by Uruguayan artist Joaquin Torres Garcia (*Inverted America*, 1943), this approach may allow accomplishing the rich rep-ertoire of the informal technologies. Typical from Brazil, Colombia,

Peru, Cuba, among other countries marked by colonialist legacies, those technologies are forged by "architectures of necessity" and address technology from the point of view of dissidence, as artist Ernesto Oroza defines in his theoretical and artistic work.

As suggested by anthropologist Eduardo Viveiros de Castro, we have a lot to learn from the Amerindians' perspectivism (Viveiros de Castro 2017), understanding, first of all, that each culture or society has its own unique perspective on the world, shaped by its history, values, beliefs, and practices. One aspect of "Amerindian perspectivism" refers to the way Indigenous peoples have a different concept of the self and the natural world than do Western societies. This leads to fundamentally different ways of understanding and interacting with the world, viewing animals and other natural phenomena as possessing their agency and consciousness, and not merely as a passive and inanimate collection of objects to be exploited and controlled.

This approach does not mean that modern forms of knowledge are unnecessary. As anthropologist Arturo Escobar argues in his famous article "Pachamamicos versus modérnicos":

> On the one hand, critical modern forms of knowledge have been beneficial, for example, in understanding domination in its materiality and ideological aspects. Nevertheless, pachammamico's knowledge could be more important today to understand what is emerging and what points toward the constitution of "worlds and knowledge" in another way. (Escobar 2011; reverse translation by the author)

This agenda is quite suggestive for thinking in different approaches to artificial intelligence beyond the human–machine opposition and its eugenic prerogatives based on conceptions of the 'standard' and the 'abnormal'. Following the not-regular and not-predictable path, such an alternative agenda points to multiple ways of seeing and worldmaking, taking what falls outside the pattern not as its model but as its point of departure.

References

Agamben, Giorgio. 2009. *O que é contemporâneo? E outros ensaios.* Trans. Vinícius Nicastro Honesko. Chapecó: Argos.

Altuncu, Enes, Virginia N. L. Franqueira, and Shujun Li. 2022. "Deepfake: Definitions, Performance Metrics and Standards, Datasets and Benchmarks, and a Meta-Review." arXiv. https://doi.org/10.48550/arXiv.2208.10913.

Appadurai, Arjun. 1996. *Cultural Dimensions of Globalization.* Minneapolis: University of Minnesota Press.

Azoulay, Ariella Aïsha. 2019. *Potential History: Unlearning Imperialism.* New York: Verso.

Beiguelman, Bernardo. 1997. "Genética, Ética e Estado: (Genetics, Ethics and State)." *Brazilian Journal of Genetics* 20, no. 3. https://doi.org/10.1590/S0100-8455199 7000300027.

Belden-Adams, Kris. 2020. *Eugenics, "Aristogenics," Photography: Picturing Privilege.* New York: Routledge.

Bostrom, N., John Harris, and J. Savulescu. 2018. "The New Eugenics of Transhuman-ism: A Feminist Assessment by Nikila Lakshmanan, Paralegal Abstract." http://genderforum.org/wp-content/uploads/2018/05/5_Lakshmanan_Transhumanism.pdf.

Bruce-Lockhart, Chelsea, Liz Faunce, and John Burn-Murdoch. "The Oscars Diversity Problem in Charts." *Financial Times,* February 7, 2020. https://www.ft.com/content/ca2e8368-48e6-11ea-aeb3-955839e06441.

Bruno, Christophe. 2006. "Logo.Hallucination." *Christophe Bruno* (blog). November 7, 2006. https://christophebruno.com/portfolio/logo-hallucination-2006/.

Buolamwini, Joy, and Timnit Gebru. 2018. "Gender Shades: Intersectional Accuracy Disparities in Commercial Gender Classification." In *Proceedings of the 1st Confer-ence on Fairness, Accountability and Transparency,* 77–91. PMLR. https://proceed-ings.mlr.press/v81/buolamwini18a.html.

Chaderjian, Daniel. 2022. "Artificial and Unreal: The Ethics of Beautification Tech-nology for Images and Social Media." *Viterbi Conversations in Ethics.* May 5, 2022. https://vce.usc.edu/volume-6-issue-1/artificial-and-unreal-the-ethics-of-beautifi cation-technology-for-images-and-social-media/.

Clark, Timothy J. 2007. *Modernismos.* Ed. Sonia Salzstein. São Paulo: Cosac & Naify.

Cole, Samantha. 2018. "Deepfakes Were Created as a Way to Own Women's Bodies—We Can't Forget That." *Vice.* June 18, 2018. https://www.vice.com/en/article/nekqmd/deepfake-porn-origins-sexism-reddit-v25n2.

Couldry, Nick, and Ulises A. Mejias. 2019. *The Costs of Connection: How Data Is Col-onizing Human Life and Appropriating It for Capitalism.* Stanford, Calif.: Stanford University Press.

Crary, Jonathan. 1991. *Techniques of the Observer: On Vision and Modernity in the Nine-teenth Century.* Cambridge, Mass: MIT Press.

Crary, Jonathan. 2000. *Suspensions of Perception: Attention, Spectacle, and Modern Culture.* 2nd. ed. Cambridge, Mass: MIT Press.

Crawford, Kate, and Trevor Paglen. 2019. "Excavating A.I." September 19, 2019. https://excavating.ai.

134 Critical Art Ensemble. 1998. *Flesh Machine; Cyborgs, Designer Babies, Eugenic Conscious-ness*. Brooklyn, N.Y.: Autonomedia.

Darwin, Charles. 1871. *On the Origin of Species*. 5th ed. New York: D. Appleton and Co. https://doi.org/10.5962/bhl.title.28875.

Darwin, Charles. 1896. *The Descent of Man, and Selection in Relation to Sex*. Vol. 2. London: John Murray.

Duster, Troy. 2003. *Backdoor to Eugenics*. 2nd ed. New York: Routledge.

Eco, Umberto. 1984. *Viagem Na Irrealidade Cotidiana*. Rio de Janeiro: NOVA FRONTEIRA.

Escobar, Arturo. 2011. "¿"Pachamámicos" versus "Modérnicos"?" *Tabula Rasa* 15:265–73.

EPIC (Electronic Privacy Information Center). 2019. "In Re HireVue." https://epic.org/documents/in-re-hirevue/.

"Eugenics Timeline." 2015. Eugenics Archives. https://eugenicsarchive.ca/discover/timeline/.

Fischer, Georg. 2019. "'Where Are the Botocudos?' Anthropological Displays and the Entanglements of Staring, 1882–1883." *História, Ciências, Saúde-Manguinhos* 26 (September): 969–92.

Fontcuberta, Joan. 2007. *Datascapes: Orogenesis/Googlegrams*. Seville, Spain: Photovision.

Foster, Hal, ed. 1998. *Vision and Visuality*. Discussions in Contemporary Culture 2. Seattle, Wash.: New Press.

Foucault, Michel. 1995. *Discipline and Punish: The Birth of the Prison*. 2nd ed. New York: Vintage.

Freire, Paulo. 2018. *Pedagogia do oprimido*. 65th ed. São Paulo: Paz & Terra.

Friedberg, Anne. 2009. *The Virtual Window—From Alberti to Microsoft*. Cambridge, Mass.: MIT Press.

Galton, Francis. 1879. "Composite Portraits Made by Combining Those of Many Differ-ent Persons into a Single Figure." *Journal of the Anthropological Institute* 8:132–48.

Galton, Francis. 1883. *Inquiries into Human Faculty*. London: Macmillan. https://galton.org/books/human-faculty/.

Galton, Francis. 1904. "Eugenics: Its Definition, Scope, and Aims." American Journal of Sociology 10 (1): 1–25. https://doi.org/10.1086/211280.

Goldenfein, Jake. 2020. "Facial Recognition Is Only the Beginning." *Public Books*. January 27, 2020. https://www.publicbooks.org/facial-recognition-is-only-the-beginning/.

Goodfellow, Ian, Yoshua Bengio, and Aaron Courville. 2016. *Deep Learning*. Cam-bridge, Mass.: MIT Press.

Grohmann, Rafael, Gabriel Pereira, Abel Guerra, Ludmila Costhek Abilio, Bruno More-schi, and Amanda Jurno. 2022. "Platform Scams: Brazilian Workers' Experiences of Dishonest and Uncertain Algorithmic Management." *New Media & Society* 24, no. 7: 1611–31. https://doi.org/10.1177/14614448221099225.

Grue, Lars, and Arvid Heiberg. 2006. "Notes on the History of Normality—Reflections on the Work of Quetelet and Galton." *Scandinavian Journal of Disability Research* 8, no. 4: 232–46. https://doi.org/10.1080/15017410600608491.

Harwell, Drew. 2019. "A Face-Scanning Algorithm Increasingly Decides Whether You Deserve the Job." *Washington Post,* November 6, 2019. https://www.washington post.com/technology/2019/10/22/ai-hiring-face-scanning-algorithm-increasingly -decides-whether-you-deserve-job/.

Hashemi, Mahdi, and Margaret Hall. 2020. "Criminal Tendency Detection from Facial Images and the Gender Bias Effect." *Journal of Big Data* 7, no. 1: 2. https://doi.org/ 10.1186/s40537-019-0282-4.

Heritable Human Genome Editing. 2020. Washington, D.C.: National Academies Press. https://doi.org/10.17226/25665.

Hui, Yuk. 2020. *Tecnodiversidade*. São Paulo, Brazil: Ubu Editora.

Huyssen, Andreas. 2009. *Seduzidos Pela Memória*. Rio de Janeiro, Brazil: AEROPLANO.

Huyssen, Andreas. 2014. *Culturas do Passado-Presente*. Rio de Janeiro, Brazil: Contraponto.

Jeudy, Henri Pierre, and Paola Berenstein. 2006. *Corpos e Cenários Urbanos. Territórios Urbanos e Políticas Culturais*. Salvador, Brazil: Edufba.

Jeudy, Henri-Pierre. 2005. *Espelho das Cidades*. Rio de Janeiro, Brazil: Casa Da Palavra.

Kantayya, Shalini, dir. 2020. *Coded Bias*. Documentary. 7th Empire Media. https:// www.codedbias.com.

Karkkainen, Kimmo, and Jungseock Joo. 2021. "FairFace: Face Attribute Dataset for Balanced Race, Gender, and Age for Bias Measurement and Mitigation." In *2021 IEEE Winter Conference on Applications of Computer Vision (WACV)*, 1547–57. Waikoloa, Hawaii: IEEE. https://doi.org/10.1109/WACV48630.2021.00159.

Karras, Tero, Samuli Laine, Miika Aittala, Janne Hellsten, Jaakko Lehtinen, and Timo Aila. 2020. "Analyzing and Improving the Image Quality of StyleGAN." In *2020 IEEE/ CVF Conference on Computer Vision and Pattern Recognition (CVPR)*, 8107–16. https:// doi.org/10.1109/CVPR42600.2020.00813.

Kember, Sarah. 2014. "Face Recognition and the Emergence of Smart Photography." *Journal of Visual Culture* 13, no. 2: 182–99. https://doi.org/10.1177/147041291 4541767.

LargoFilms. 2020. "Henry Cavill Selected as the Next Bond by Largo.Aix." LargoFilms. September 6, 2020. http://largofilms.ch/henry-cavill-swaps-his-cape-for-a-martini -in-ai-victory-as-the-next-bond/.

Lee-Morrison, Lila. 2019. *Portraits of Automated Facial Recognition: On Machinic Ways of Seeing the Face*. Bielefeld: transcript. https://doi.org/10.14361/9783839448465.

Leroi, Armand Marie. 2005. *Mutants: On Genetic Variety and the Human Body*. New York: Penguin Books.

Machado, Maria Helena Pereira Toledo, and Sasha Huber, eds. 2010. *(T)races of Louis Agassiz: Photography, Body and Science, Yesterday and Today / Rastros e raças de Louis Agassiz: fotografía, corpo e ciência, ontem e hoje*. Rio de Janeiro, Brasil: Capacete Entretenimentos.

Manovich, Lev. 2014. "Selfiexploratory." *Sefiecity*. http://selfiecity.net/selfiexploratory/.

McQuillan, Dan. 2022. *Resisting A.I.: An Anti-Fascist Approach to Artificial Intelligence*. Bristol, UK: Bristol University Press.

Moreschi, Bruno, Gabriel Pereira, Fabio Gagliardi Cozman, and Gustavo Aires Tiago.

2020. "The Brazilian Workers in Amazon Mechanical Turk: Dreams and Realities of Ghost Workers." *Contracampo* 39, no. 1: 1–21.

Noble, Safiya Umoja. 2018. *Algorithms of Oppression: How Search Engines Reinforce Racism*. New York: NYU Press.

Nordstrom, Byron J. 2019. "Eugenics in the Nordic Countries." *Nordics.Info*. September 24, 2019. https://nordics.info/show/artikel/eugenics-in-the-nordic -countries.

Novak, Daniel. 2004. "A Model Jew: 'Literary Photographs' and the Jewish Body in Daniel Deronda." *Representations* 85, no. 1: 58–97. https://doi.org/10.1525/ rep.2004.85.1.58.

Owens, Kellie, and Alexis Walker. 2020. "Those Designing Healthcare Algorithms Must Become Actively Anti-Racist." *Nature Medicine* 26, no. 9: 1327–28. https://doi .org/10.1038/s41591-020-1020-3.

Panetta, Francesca, and Halsey Burgund, dirs. 2020. *In Event of Moon Disaster*. https:// vimeo.com/439750398.

Pasquinelli, Mateo, and Vladan Joler. 2020. "The Nooscope Manifested: Artificial Intelligence as Instrument of Knowledge Extractivism." KIM research group (Karlsruhe University of Arts and Design) and Share Lab (Novi Sad). https://nooscope.ai.

Pelbart, Peter Pal. 2007. "Tempos agonísticos." In *Sentidos da Arte Contemporânea: Seminários Internacionais Vale do Rio Doce* 2:68–79. Vila Velha, Brazil: Suzy Muniz Produções. https://www.estantevirtual.com.br/redstarteodoro/ fernando-pessoa-katia-canton-sentidos-e-arte-contemporanea-367675714.

Pereira, Gabriel, Bruno Moreschi, André Mintz, and Giselle Beiguelman. "We've Always Been Antagonistic: Algorithmic Resistances and Dissidences beyond the Global North." *Media International Australia* 183, no. 1 (May 2022): 124–38. https:// doi.org/10.1177/1329878X221074792.

Rancière, Jacques. 2004. *The Politics of Aesthetics: The Distribution of the Sensible*. London: Continuum.

Reynolds, Simon. 2012. *Retromania: Pop Culture's Addiction to Its Own Past*. New York: Faber & Faber.

Rowland, Mary. 2022. "Online Visual Self-Presentation: Augmented Reality Face Filters, Selfie-Editing Behaviors, and Body Image Disorder." *Journal of Research in Gender Studies* 12, no. 1: 99–114. https://doi.org/10.22381/JRGS12120227.

Schwarcz, Lilia Moritz. 1999. *The Spectacle of the Races: Scientists, Institutions, and the Race Question in Brazil, 1870–1930*. Trans. Lilia Guyer. New York: Hill and Wang.

Sekula, Allan. 1986. "The Body and the Archive." *October* 39: 3–64. https://doi.org/ 10.2307/778312.

Shapira, Shahak. 2017. "Yolocaust—The Aftermath." http://yolocaust.de.

Shaw, Laura. n.d. "Gregory Stock Publishes *Redesigning Humans: Our Inevitable Genetic Future*." The Eugenics Archives. Accessed January 6, 2023. http://eugenicsarchive .ca/discover/timeline/5173222aeed5c60000000046.

Silva, Tarcízio da. 2022. *Racismo algorítmico: Inteligência artificial e discriminação nas redes digitais*. São Paulo, Brazil: Edições Sesc SP.

Silva, Tarcízio da, André Mintz, Janna Joceli Omena, Beatrice Gobbo, Taís Oliveira,

Helen Tatiana Takamitsu, Elena Pilipets, and Hamdan Azhar. 2020. "APIs de Visão Computacional: investigando mediações algorítmicas a partir de estudo de bancos de imagens." *Logos* 27, no. 1. https://doi.org/10.12957/logos.2020.51523.

Steed, Ryan, and Aylin Caliskan. 2021. "Image Representations Learned with Unsupervised Pre-Training Contain Human-like Biases." In *Proceedings of the 2021 ACM Conference on Fairness, Accountability, and Transparency,* 701–13. Virtual Event Canada: ACM. https://doi.org/10.1145/3442188.3445932.

Stock, Gregory. 2002. Redesigning Humans: Our Inevitable Genetic Future. Boston: Houghton Mifflin Harcourt, 2002.

Stone, Karen. 2019. "Sterilization of Indigenous Women in Canada | The Canadian Encyclopedia." In *The Canadian Enciclopedia.* https://www.thecanadianencyclopedia .ca/en/article/sterilization-of-indigenous-women-in-canada.

Szeliski, Richard. 2011. *Computer Vision.* Texts in Computer Science. London: Springer London. https://doi.org/10.1007/978-1-84882-935-0.

"This Person Does Not Exist." 2018. Accessed March 2, 2021. https://thispersondoes notexist.com/.

Turing, Alan M. 1950. "Computing Machinery and Intelligence." *Mind* 59, no. 236: 433–60. https://doi.org/10.1093/mind/LIX.236.433.

Virilio, Paul, Bertrand Richard, and Ames Hodges. 2012. *The Administration of Fear.* Los Angeles, Calif.: Semiotext.

Viveiros de Castro, Eduardo. 2017. *Cannibal Metaphysics.* Trans. and ed. Peter Skafish. Minneapolis: University of Minnesota Press.

Wang, Yilun, and Michal Kosinski. 2018. "Deep Neural Networks Are More Accurate Than Humans at Detecting Sexual Orientation from Facial Images." *Journal of Personality and Social Psychology* 114, no. 2: 246. https://doi.org/10.1037/pspa 0000098.

Wegenstein, Bernadette. 2012. *The Cosmetic Gaze: Body Modification and the Construction of Beauty.* Cambridge, Mass: MIT Press.

Wilson, Robert A. 2017. *The Eugenic Mind Project.* Cambridge, Mass.: The MIT Press.

Wolstenholme, G. E. W. (Gordon Ethelbert Ward) and Ciba Foundation. 1963. *Man and His Future; A Ciba Foundation Volume.* Boston: Little Brown. http://archive.org/ details/manhisfutureciba00wols.

Wu, Xiaolin, and Xi Zhang. 2016. "Automated Inference on Criminality Using Face Images." ArXiv. November. https://www.semanticscholar.org/paper/1cd357b675 a659413e8abf2eafad2a463272a85f.

Zer-Aviv, Mushon. 2018. "The Normalizing Machine | An Experiment in Machine Learning & Algorithmic Prejudice." http://mushon.com/tnm/.

Zou, James, and Londa Schiebinger. 2018. "A.I. Can Be Sexist and Racist—It's Time to Make It Fair." *Nature* 559 (7714): 324–26. https://doi.org/10.1038/d41586-018 -05707-8.

Zylinska, Joanna. 2017. *Nonhuman Photography: Theories, Histories, Genres.* Cambridge, Mass.: MIT Press.

Authors

Giselle Beiguelman is an artist and associate professor in the faculty of architecture, urbanism, and design at the University of São Paulo. She is the author of *Políticas da Imagem: Vigilância e Resistência na Dadosfera Politics* (Politics of the image: surveillance and resistance in the datasphere), among others. Her artistic works are part of museum collections in Brazil and abroad, including ZKM (Germany), Jewish Museum Berlin, and Pinacoteca de São Paulo.

Melody Devries is a PhD candidate and digital ethnographer at Toronto Metropolitan University studying how users construct political worlds online. She is coeditor of *Rise of the Far-Right: Technologies of Recruitment and Mobilization,* has recently published in the *Canadian Journal of Communication*, and is currently editing a special issue with *Big Data & Society.*

Winnie Soon is an artist and course leader/senior lecturer at Creative Computing Institute, University of the Arts London, as well as associate professor at Aarhus University. Their latest coauthored books are *Aesthetic Programming: A Handbook of Software Studies* and *Fix My Code,* intersecting critical art and technology practices.

Magdalena Tyżlik-Carver is associate professor of digital communication and culture in the Department of Digital Design and Information Studies at Aarhus University and curator of digital art and design. Her recent curatorial projects include the exhibitions *Fermenting Data: Aarhus 8000-8220* (2021) and *Screenshots: Desire and Automated Image* (2019). She is coeditor of *Executing Practices*.